A GUIDE
CONTINENTAL CURRENCY AND COINS

A Numismatic Study and Guide to Collecting

Q. David Bowers

Research Associates
Julia H. Casey, Ray Williams
Valuations Editor
Bruce Hagen
Foreword by
Christopher R. McDowell

Whitman Publishing, LLC
PUBLISHING SINCE 1934

Whitman .com

A GUIDE BOOK OF
CONTINENTAL
CURRENCY AND COINS

© 2021 Whitman Publishing, LLC
1974 Chandalar Drive, Suite D, Pelham, AL 35124

THE OFFICIAL RED BOOK is a trademark of Whitman Publishing, LLC.

Correspondence concerning this book may be directed to
Whitman Publishing, Attn: Continental Currency, at the address above.

ISBN: 0794848400
Printed in China

Disclaimer: Expert opinion should be sought in any significant numismatic purchase. This book is presented as a guide only. No warranty or representation of any kind is made concerning the completeness of the information presented. The author, a professional numismatist, regularly buys, sells, and holds certain of the items discussed in this book.

Caveat: The value estimates given are subject to variation and differences of opinion. Before making decisions to buy or sell, consult the latest information. Past performance of the rare-coin market or any coin or series within that market is not necessarily an indication of future performance, as the future is unknown. Such factors as changing demand, popularity, grading interpretations, strength of the overall coin market, and economic conditions will continue to be influences.

Whitman Publishing is a leading publisher of numismatic reference books, supplies, and storage and display products that help you build, appreciate, and share great collections. To browse our complete catalog, visit Whitman Publishing online at www.Whitman.com.

If you enjoy this book, we invite you to learn more about America's history by starting a new coin collection and reading as much as possible.

You can join the American Numismatic Association (ANA), the nation's largest hobby group for coin collectors. Collect coins and other currency, learn about numismatics, and make new friends in the hobby. Explore the ANA at www.Money.org.

Whitman®

Contents

FOREWORD

This book brings together all of the national currency and coins of the American Revolutionary period in one place for the first time. The diversity of numismatic materials produced during this time in our nation's history is unequalled. It was a time of bold experimentation in everything from paper to designs. Nothing was yet fixed; every motto, legend, image, and word was new and significant. Some ideas were better than others, but practicality and the exigencies of the moment often, but not always, held sway over beauty. The May 10, 1775, $20 Continental Currency bill with marbled border is one of the most beautiful and fascinating pieces in American numismatics. Anyone looking at the swirling red, blue, and yellow shades of its marbled edge, with authentic signatures and a unique motto selected by Benjamin Franklin himself, knows it is something special. But it was gone in a flash, never to be repeated as Congress struggled to keep expenses in line as the war raged around them. All later currency was printed on paper produced regionally. Each bill and each coin of this era tells a special story of our forefathers' fight for independence and liberty. No aspect of American numismatics is more deserving of our time and effort than what appears within these pages. This is the genesis of all that followed and there is no better guide on the tour through this special subject than Q. David Bowers.

I am the editor of the *Journal of Early American Numismatics*, formerly the *Colonial Newsletter*, a publication of the American Numismatic Society. I had known of Dave Bowers for decades before I met him, but we were personally introduced after I wrote an article on Daniel Van Voorhees, an eighteenth-century New York silversmith involved in the production of Vermont copper coinage of the 1785 to 1788 period. Dave contacted the publisher to ask if he could have a special copy of my article, which I agreed to. From that day to now we have corresponded weekly, sometimes daily, regarding colonial numismatics. Although Dave's interest extends beyond American colonial numismatics, the coins and currency of the Revolutionary period have always been of special interest to him since the 1950s. He has been involved in the sale of the finest colonial collections ever assembled and has known most of the great collectors of the twentieth century, but Dave is also a scholar. He has written and sold more books than any other numismatic author past or present. His books are both popular and influential.

What is the secret sauce that makes his books so popular? That is the question I asked myself when he first made me aware he was working on this project.

Fortunately, I was permitted to be part of the action and watch as the manuscript moved from concept to physical book. Through this experience I gained valuable insight into how Dave operates. He is without a doubt the current "Dean of American Numismatics," and it was indeed a privilege to get an inside look.

The first ingredient in Dave's secret sauce is a great topic. This book fills a void—a gap in our numismatic knowledge that screams to be filled by a single, easily available study. For reasons that will never be clear to me, numismatists have in the past segregated currency from coins in written works. Even at auctions, colonial currency is sold in one room and coins in another. Last year I strode into an auction in Baltimore to take my seat when a friend approached me to say I must be lost, as they were auctioning colonial currency in that room and the colonial coin auction was in the next room over. Why can't both be in the same room? Why can't both be in the same book? Certainly our forefathers did not reserve one pocket for paper and the other for silver. Both circulated together, and both should be studied and enjoyed together. This book does that. It brings into one place both paper currency and coins, the way things were meant to be.

The second ingredient is superb research. Dave's unparalleled numismatic knowledge is, of course, a huge advantage, but no single person can know everything. So, he has gathered many friends around him who are experts in a wide range of subjects. When he comes across a topic where he knows someone else has been conducting research, he contacts that person to learn what's new. As Dave put together this book, he contacted dozens of experts to ask questions. In this way, he made sure that what he wrote was correct and up to date. The world of colonial and early American numismatics is in a state of flux. New ideas and theories are questioning and sometimes upending many of the concepts that were once considered established dogma. Take, for example, the Continental dollar coin. In the past five years our view of this coinage has changed considerably. In writing this book, Dave contacted all the major players in the current debate over the origin of this coinage and synthesized their thoughts and writings; however, he did not just parrot back other's thoughts, but he analyzed everything and made it his own. This same process was repeated over and over as this book moved forward to completion. Dave strives to get it right and plugs away until he does. Thus, I can say that this book brings forth the most up-to-date and accurate information available in any single book on the topic of Revolutionary-era paper currency and coins.

The third ingredient is readability. Many of the topics contained in this book are complex, but Dave has a way of making everything easy to understand. In this way his works can be enjoyed by both the novice collector and the advanced numismatist. In preparing this book, Dave was particularly struck by the fact that Congress forced its ever-depreciating bills on the public. That is, as the value of Continental bills began to decline from over-production, counterfeiting, and hyper-inflation, Congress began to require, under penalty of law, that unwilling merchants accept them at face value. Those who refused were labelled Tories and subject to all sorts of deprivation, ridicule, or worse. This totalitarianism is not an account printed in our history books, but it is a fact brought to life in these pages. The hidden story of these bills and coins is an important and underappreciated aspect of this nation's founding. By gaining a fuller understanding of this topic, we can better appreciate the struggles of the Revolutionary era.

Part of readability in numismatics is having great illustrations. All of Dave's books, including this one, contain images of the very finest bills and coins available. Dave is able to draw from his own collection, the library of Stack's Bowers Galleries, and selected private sources to bring to the reader the best of the best. These images enhance the experience like nothing else can. There are hundreds of images in this book.

The final ingredient is setting an available price point without skimping on quality. Far too many of the numismatic books published today cost on the far side of $100 and are thus of small print runs and are seen by a relatively restricted audience. Dave strives to price his books at a level that makes them accessible to the general public. This is nowhere more evident than with the present publisher: Whitman Publishing, which has issued dozens of his titles and editions. At the same time, all of his books are nicely bound, with fine paper, and include beautiful color images. As a general rule, books such as this are not read and thrown away, but rather purchased with the intent to be placed on a bookshelf and enjoyed over a lifetime. Thus, it is important that the book be a quality product especially designed to last and be displayed for years to come. Dave's extensive experience in publishing makes it possible for him to create and have others publish a very high-quality product at a price everyone can afford.

The current book includes all the ingredients that make for a super numismatic publication. After reading the *Guide Book of Continental Currency and Coins* you will have a much greater understanding and appreciation not only of the currency and coins of the Revolutionary period, but also of the hardships faced by our forefathers in shaping this great nation.

Christopher R. McDowell
Cincinnati, Ohio

Christopher R. McDowell studied history and political science while enlisted in the U.S. Army, graduating with a bachelor's degree from Marshall University in West Virginia. He earned his J.D. at West Virginia University College of Law, after which he served as an Army officer overseas in the JAG Corps. Today McDowell is an attorney focusing on criminal and commercial-related litigation as well as real-estate transactions. As editor of the *Colonial Newsletter* (and now the *Journal of Early American Numismatics*), he assists other researchers in uncovering the mysteries and correcting the record of our numismatic past, as well as conducting his own extensive research and writing.

PUBLISHER'S PREFACE

As a publisher and a numismatist, I'm always on the lookout for "coin books" that can leap from the hobbyist world of antiques and collectibles into the bigger river of mainstream American history. This goal is more elusive than you might expect. But the potential is always there, because the pleasures of coin collecting and the pleasures of studying history are so closely related.

If you're an active collector of old coins, paper money, tokens, and medals, you appreciate the connections between these objects and the broad tapestry of our national story. They're fundamental pieces of *material culture*—a scholarly term for the physical objects, resources, and architecture that surround us and define us (things that help us survive, that aid our labor, that create an identity, that solidify social relationships, etc.). Coins and paper money have been used in North America day in and day out for generations, going back to the colonial era. They're as intimately connected to American life as are newspapers, family portraits, silverware, and letters mailed back home. History you can hold in your hand, as it has been said.

The study of coins and currency is part of the art and science of numismatics. The wider discipline covers the study of all aspects of money, as well as other payment media and systems (such as barter) that humans have used to settle debts and exchange goods. Numismatics involves other social sciences: economics, quantitative and qualitative economic history, political science, and the like. Its scope also includes mining, metallurgy, mechanics, and other hard sciences and technology that go into the physical creation of coins and printing on paper. It includes design, sculpture, engraving, and fine arts similarly involved in making coins and bank notes. For a numismatist, a coin is much more than just a coin! It's an artifact of its times. It has a lot to tell about the people who created it, and those who used it.

In our fast-paced world, historians as a general class rarely get the credit they deserve for helping us understand the past (and thereby the present). This has been changing in recent years, and it's gratifying to watch as serious history grows into a popular consumable. A case study relevant to the subject of this book: Lin-Manuel Miranda's 2015 smash-hit musical *Hamilton*, itself based on historian Ron Chernow's award-winning 2004 book *Alexander Hamilton*, about the Founding Father who created the nation's financial system and was our first Treasury secretary.

The entertaining packaging of history is perhaps good and bad for numismatics. On the one hand, anything that popularizes history—assuming it's well researched and balanced—is good for elevating knowledge overall, and has the potential to spark interest in history's many highways and byways, including all manner of material culture. On the other hand, with so much entertainingly produced history available, in so many easily accessible formats (television, movies, online videos, even Broadway musicals), a quieter avenue like coin-collecting might get lost on the map. Numismatics, misunderstood, could run the risk of being sidelined as a narrow specialty—one where you "learn more and more about less and less, until you know everything about nothing"—rather than being appreciated as a permeating science that touches every aspect of American life.

As the subtitle of author Todd Andrlik's 2012 book *Reporting the Revolutionary War* says, "Before it was history, it was news." This applies to money as much as anything, and it's important to remember that before coins and paper currency became historical collectibles, they were new, freshly minted or printed, often experimental, and, during the American fight for independence, a vibrant act of revolution themselves. Capturing that energy and sense of uncharted newness, while bringing order to its complexity, is a challenge. Among American historians, none is so qualified to write about the money of the American Revolutionary War as Q. David Bowers. His work in the field, which started in the 1950s, is innovative, prolific, and ongoing.

With more than fifty books to his credit, Bowers ranks among the greats of our nation's historians—those who have lifted high the lamp of knowledge. Certainly in the field of economic history he is a unique, and uniquely productive, author.

Bowers has anecdotally told the story of a well-known Civil War historian he chatted with after a lecture. He asked the expert what he knew about Civil War money. The reply was, essentially, "I know that Confederate currency was nearly worthless before the end of the conflict." No deep knowledge of the wartime birth of new banking systems, no intimacy with the way the nation's biggest military mobilization was financed. On the level of day-to-day life during the war, he could share nothing of, for example, the vital role played by little bronze tokens minted in the tens of millions by hundreds of private businessmen. Were those tokens "money"? Were they crucially important to Americans during the early 1860s? Yes and yes! "Civil War tokens" fueled the engine of daily commerce after all legal-tender federal coins—not just gold and silver, but even lowly copper cents—were hoarded by a fearful and war-weary public. Knowledge of this sort goes beyond valuing coins and currency as "collectibles." It gets to the heart of their true worth, as artifacts of the American experience.

In the *Guide Book of Continental Currency and Coins*, Dave Bowers has written a volume that bridges the gap between numismatics and mainstream history. He provides a fresh understanding of the American Revolution using numismatics as his lens. For many readers this will be radical and new. History buffs who know the battles, the generals, and the politics will now also understand the financial and economic forces of the Revolution. This is not a dusty math lesson or a lecture on the "dismal science" of economics. Rather, it's a fascinating exploration of national-level financial experimentation, as well as the day-to-day monetary life of Americans, both Tory and revolutionary.

How was Continental Currency produced; how were the notes distributed? Who signed them? Before all that, how were they even *authorized*—when the Continental Congress had no traditional foundation for a paper-money issue, no gold or silver to back up the paper and ink? How could Congress raise money to fight a war that was partially enflamed by tax collection? How strong was the promise to redeem the paper after the war? Such a promise would require an unruly volunteer army to conquer the greatest military force on earth!

The human stories that emerge are sometimes funny, sometimes terrifying, and always enlightening. Did a New Yorker really wallpaper his rooms with Continental Currency during the war? How did General Washington threaten those who refused to accept the money as payment for goods? What happened to Quakers who, for religious reasons, refused to handle the paper money? What were Spanish silver dollars, and how did they figure into the emerging economy? How did the eccentric Massachusetts businessman "Lord" Timothy Dexter make a fortune speculating in war debt and Continental Currency? Some facts are surprising, and rarely covered in histories of the Revolution—for example, it was illegal during the war to say anything negative about the new paper money, and many Americans were jailed for public criticism, a concept that would be unthinkable to later generations. Bowers shares and comments on newspaper accounts from both sides of the conflict, some neutrally reporting the monetary news of the day, some degrading the "dirty trash" currency. He tells of citizens "burnt in the brawn of the left thumb" for the crime of passing counterfeit money—and even being executed for the "pernicious tendency."

On the artistic and technical side, Bowers lays out the designs and rich symbolism used on Continental Currency notes. He tells how they were printed, and the ingenious techniques employed to frustrate counterfeiters. And he tells of Benjamin Franklin and others who influenced the look and feel of the new money.

For collectors, he describes how to grade Continental Currency—a factor crucial to valuation. He gives rarity ratings, typical prices in multiple grades, and advice on market conditions.

He explores the enigmatic Continental dollar coins (or are they medals?), laying out a couple hundred years of research and speculation, including startling recent theories based on new research and insights.

Within the discipline of numismatic history, Q. David Bowers has no peers. He's extremely productive, he's popularized the field and connected it to other social sciences, and he's influential and inspirational to other researchers. The *Guide Book of Continental Currency and Coins* adds to his standing among American historians, and continues to elevate the status of numismatics as a serious branch of American history, as important as the popular works of Benson Lossing or Barbara Tuchman or David McCullough—a companion to presidential and other political history, social-movement history, military history, and every other highway and byway that history buffs happily explore.

Dennis Tucker
Publisher, Whitman Publishing, LLC

INTRODUCTION

Continental money of both kinds—notes and coins—has fascinated me for a long time. My involvement in dealing in Continental Currency and Continental dollars in the 1950s led me to read many books on the history of the era, including Benson J. Lossing's encyclopedic two-volume *Field-Book of the American Revolution* and the peripheral *Timothy Dexter Revisited*, by John P. Marquand, published in 1960. Soon after reading the latter, I went to Newburyport to visit the Dexter mansion on High Street and, courtesy of the owner, explored the beautiful building and grounds. The surrounding land was much smaller than depicted on engravings. At one time Dexter was one of the most interesting and enigmatic figures in town, with life-size statues of historical figures in the front yard (a few survive and have been restored). As I relate in this book, the source of Dexter's fortune remains somewhat of a mystery, but it was most likely arrived at by speculation in federal and state Revolutionary War debt and Continental Currency, the latter of which could be purchased for as low as $1,000 in paper for $1 in coins, and he later redeemed it at 100 to 1, still later changed to 40 to 1 after the federal government, under our current Constitution, instituted that redemption policy.

Along the way I formed a collection of bills by issue date and denomination, except for several that eluded me, including the 1775 $20 on French paper. I

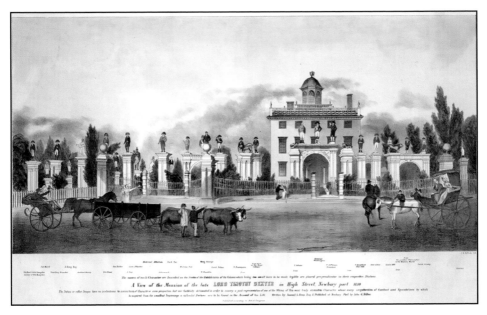

Timothy Dexter's mansion in Newburyport with statues of historical figures in the front.

found the inscriptions and mottoes, which I first came across in the J.W. Scott Stamp & Coin Company *Standard Catalogue No. 2, Paper Money*, 1889, to be absolutely fascinating. The continuing research of Eric P. Newman, a fine friend from my teenage years onward, kept adding new information. A researcher par excellence, Newman's works were factual rather than theoretical or guesswork, needing little later revision.

My experience with Continental dollar coins has been extensive. Over the years I have bought and sold all of the die combinations. A favorite was the 1776 coin with CURRENCEY spelled correctly by redoing the last two letters and adding an ornament. Among these was the coin in the Emery May Norweb Collection that was sold to Eric Newman.

Eric was almost alone in his in-depth research into Continental dollars until the last decade of the twentieth century, when Michael Hodder's "The Continental Currency Coinage of 1776: A Trial Die and Metallic Emission Sequence" was published by the American Numismatic Association in 1991. This treated emission sequences, weights, and other data in a manner that had not been done before. I have adapted extensive citations from his study and used them in chapter 6. At the time Michael was on the staff of Bowers and Merena Galleries in Wolfeboro, New Hampshire. In 1993 he, along with a small group of others, founded the Colonial Coin Collectors Club (C4), which grew to include today's hundreds of members and to publish multiple reference books.

In the second decade of the present century the coins attracted a new wave of attention, especially as to where and how they were minted and distributed. In my opinion, the situation has been excellently synopsized in John M. Kleeberg's study, "The Continental Dollar; British Medals or American Coins?" published in the *Journal of Early American Numismatics* in December 2018. By then, other researchers including Bill Eckberg, Erik Goldstein, David McCarthy, and Maureen Levine had published other theories, mainly that the coins were in fact medals and had been made in Europe. As this book goes to press, the debate continues.

While the Continental Currency bills and Continental dollar coins have always fascinated me, the history concerning them has been an even greater attraction. The advent of the Internet has made it possible for me and others to do research with an ease that was not achievable earlier. No longer do I have to go to the American Antiquarian Society, the Library of Congress, and other institutions to fill out call slips and wait for a group of books to arrive. A few

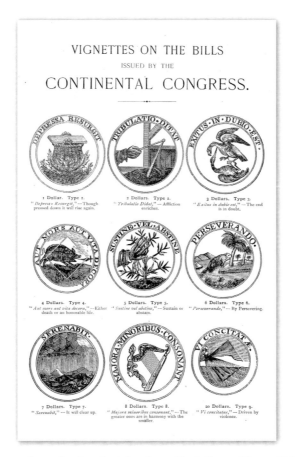

A page from the *Standard Catalogue No. 2, Paper Money*, **1889.**

keystrokes make thousands of books, newspaper articles, and other sources available. In recent times I have gathered together my research notes dating back to the 1950s, arranged them in some semblance of order, and added much new information. If prompted I could create books on many subjects in fairly short order—say several months—by updating this information with modern Internet searches.

It is my hope that you will find this book not only a useful guide to studying and perhaps collecting Continental Currency and coins, but also to enjoy reading about their history. I found the new (to me) information on the tyrannical restrictions that Congress placed on even discussing the depreciation of paper money to be especially remarkable.

Enjoy!

Q. David Bowers
Wolfeboro, New Hampshire

Continental Congress leaders John Adams, Gouverneur Morris, Alexander Hamilton, and Thomas Jefferson.

A. THOLEY, PINX.

JOHN ADAMS. MORRIS. HAMILTON. JEFFERSON.

LEADERS OF THE CONTINENTAL CONGRE

Part I

Continental Currency Bills 1775–1779

An illustration of various Continental Currency notes.

I
A History and Overview of the Notes

On May 10, 1775, the Continental Congress—the provisional national government organized among the colonies—authorized the issuance of paper money. The seeds of the American Revolution had been sown in recent years with resistance to the Stamp Act, the Boston Tea Party, and other protests against British rule. The armed encounter between American patriots and British troops at Lexington and Concord, Massachusetts, in April 1775 brought to the fore the hostility that had been felt by American patriots for a long time and launched the Revolutionary War.

The April 1775 battle between the British troops and American patriots in Lexington, Massachusetts, marked the start of military action in the Revolutionary War.

The conflict would drag on until the surrender of British forces at Yorktown, Virginia, in 1781 and the treaty of peace in 1783. In the meantime, the outcome was uncertain, British troops occupied New York City for several years, and General George Washington's Continental Army endured many hardships.

The members of the Continental Congress had high hopes but had no reserve of precious metal or coins to provide backing for the authorized paper money. Moreover, Congress also did not have the power to levy taxes and was entirely dependent upon the states for revenue. Since the war was being fought over taxation, it was hard, if not impossible, for even the states to raise sufficient money through direct taxes. As a result, Continental paper money was backed by nothing other than a future promise that one day, when the rag-tag Continental Army defeated the greatest military on earth, the money might be properly backed. Still, the program went forward.

THE FIRST ISSUE AUTHORIZED

On June 22, 1775, Congress passed a resolution giving details for the first issue, beginning with:

> *Resolved*, That a sum not exceeding two millions of Spanish milled dollars be emitted by the Congress in bills of credit for the defense of America.
>
> That the twelve confederated colonies [excluding Georgia, discussed further below] be pledged for the redemption of bills of credit now directed to be emitted for the defense of America.

On June 23 a resolution gave the denominations to be issued as $1 to $8 in the quantity of 40,000 bills for each, plus 11,800 $20 bills, for a total of $2 million. It was further resolved that Messrs. Andrew Adams, John Rutledge, James Duane, Benjamin Franklin, and James Wilson would be a committee to get proper plates engraved, to procure the paper, and to arrange with printers to produce the bills.

On July 21 it was resolved that Richard Bache, Stephen Paschal, and Michael Hillegas would be appointed to supervise the printing and care of the currency produced. On July 25 it was decreed that a further sum equal to one million Spanish milled dollars be issued in bills of the $30 denomination. Further:

> As the signing of a great number of bills as has been directed to be issued by this Congress will require more time than the members can possibly devote to that business, consistent with the attention due to the public service,

Resolved, That the following gentlemen be appointed and authorized to sign the same, viz. Luke Morris, Samuel Meredith, Judah Foulke, Samuel Morris, Frederick Kuhl, Robert Shettle Jones, Thomas Coombe, Ellis Lewis, John Mease, Thomas Lawrence, Daniel Clymer, Thomas Barclay, John Bayard, William Craig, Thomas Barlow, John Shee, Isaac Hazelhurst [*sic*], Robert Roberts, Anthony Morris, Mordecai Lewis, George Mifflin, Robert Tuckniss, Andrew Bunner, William Jackson, Joseph Sims, James Milligan, and James Read.

That each gentleman who signs the Continental bills be allowed and paid out of the Continental Treasury one dollar and one third of a dollar for each and every thousand bills signed and numbered by him.

That the gentlemen appointed to number and sign the bills do give this receipt for the same, expressing the number & denomination of them, and after numbering and signing them shall deliver the same to the Continental treasurers, and taking their receipt for the bills so delivered.

On July 29 it was resolved that Michael Hillegas and George Clymer be the joint treasurers of the United Colonies, that they were to reside in Philadelphia, and that they give surety bonds in the amount of one hundred thousand dollars for the faithful performance of their duties, such bonds to be delivered to John Hancock, Henry Middletown, John Dickinson, John Alsop, Thomas Lynch, Richard Henry Lee, and James Wilson for the benefit of the United Colonies.

It was further resolved that twelve of the colonies (Georgia was not listed[1]) provide legislation to ensure that they pay to the United Colonies, in proportion to their population ("according to the number of inhabitants of all ages, including negroes and mulattoes, in each colony"), $2 million in four installments beginning on the last day of November 1779 and continuing to the last day of November 1782.

CONTINUATION OF THE CURRENCY

The Congress forced citizens to use Continental Currency, even though within the first year it had depreciated in relation to gold and silver coins. Many actions were taken against those who would not trade in these bills. The action of the Norwalk (Connecticut) Committee on August 6, 1776, is typical of many such punishments:

Whereas Cornelius Dyckman, of Norwalk, has been complained of to this Committee, for endeavouring to depreciate the Continental currency, emitted by the honourable Continental Congress; this Committee gave the said Dyckman the usual notice of six days, previous to their meeting this day, to answer to the charge, but the said Dyckman did not appear; whereupon this Committee proceeded to examine the evidence, by whom it appeared that the said Dyckman openly, and in a concourse of people, declared and offered to give one hundred dollars in Continental currency for ninety dollars in silver; this he did repeatedly in the course of his conversation, and at different times, adding reproachful reflections on the institutions of Committees of Observation. Whereupon this Committee, considering the high importance of supporting the credit of the Continental currency, by which the expense of Our military operations are in a great

A Revolutionary War–era broadside condemning a man for his support of the British.

measure defrayed, are of opinion that the said Dyckman did it with a design to depreciate the said currency, and thereby injure the cause of liberty, and oppose and counteract the operations of the United States in support of their invaded rights. Therefore, this Committee

Resolve, That it is evident to them that the said Dyckman is an open and malicious enemy to the proceedings of the United States in the noble stand they have made in defending their rights and repelling their enemies; and as such they publish him, requesting all persons to refrain all dealings and intercourse with said Dyckman.[2]

By order of the Committee.

THE OCCUPATION OF NEW YORK CITY

On August 27, 1776, the patriot army was defeated by the British in the Battle of Long Island, which led to the occupation of New York City, a severe blow. About 1,200 patriots were captured by the British and imprisoned in churches in Brooklyn, Flatbush, New Utrecht, and Flatlands, and some were kept on board British ships, including the notorious *Jersey* moored off of Brooklyn.

Committee Chamber, New-York, April 29, 1775.

Extract of the Proceedings of the General Committee of Observation.

Resolved unanimously,

THAT in the Opinion of this Committee, no Violence or Molestation should be offered to the Troops now quartered in this City, while they continue to behave peaceably.

By Order of the Committee,

ISAAC LOW, Chairman.

A broadside printing of the resolve of non-violence toward British troops quartered in New York, April 29, 1775.

Two different depictions of the Continental Army and
artillery retreating from Long Island in 1776, which led to
the British occupation of New York until 1783.

Interior view of the *Jersey*, a British prison ship during
the Revolutionary War, showing prisoners and a guard.

The *Jersey* prison ship on an 1859
medalet by George H. Lovett, No. 5 in
Augustus B. Sage's "Historical Tokens" series.

Following this, the British arrested patriots in the city, bringing the total of prisoners to about 5,000. The Sugar House, King's College (today's Columbia), Brick house, New Bridewell, old City Hall, North and Middle Dutch churches, and the new jail were added to the list of prisons. Health care ranged from minimal to none, food rations were sparse, and many became ill or died.

The Sugar House was one of several prisons used by the British to confine patriots during the 1776–1783 occupation of New York City.

In *The Pictorial Field-Book of the American Revolution*, Benson J. Lossing told of one such facility:

Next to the provost prison, the sugar-house in Liberty Street was most noted for the sufferings of captive patriots. It was a dark stone building, five stories in height, with small deep windows like portholes, giving it the appearance of a prison. Each story was divided into two apartments. A large, barred door opened upon Liberty Street, and from another, on the southeast side, a stair-way led to gloomy cellars, which were used as dungeons. Around the whole building was a passage a few feet wide, and there, day and night, British and Hessian sentinels patrolled. The whole was enclosed by a wooden fence nine feet in height. Within this gloomy jail the healthy and the sick, white and black, were indiscriminately thrust; and there, during the summer of 1777, many died from want of exercise, cleanliness, and fresh air. 'In the suffocating heat of summer,' says Dunlap, 'I saw every aperture of those strong walls filled with human heads, face above face, seeking a portion of the external air.' . . .

"At length, in July 1777, a jail fever was created, and great numbers died. During its prevalence the prisoners were marched out in companies of twenty, to breathe the fresh air for half an hour, while those within divided themselves into parties of six each, and there alternately enjoyed the privilege of standing 10 minutes at the windows. They had no seats, and their beds of straw were filled with vermin. They might have exchanged this horrid tenement for the comfortable quarters of a British soldier by enlisting in the king's service, but very few would thus yield their principles. They each preferred to be among the dozen bodies which were daily carried out in carts and cast into the ditches and morasses beyond the city limits. . . ."

It is important to mention that British soldiers and Hessian mercenary soldiers that were captured by the Continental Army were also kept in sordid conditions, such as in the Newgate Prison deep underground in an abandoned copper mine in Simsbury, Connecticut. Many Tory loyalists were also imprisoned and kept under miserable conditions. Neither side had the people or facilities to improve the situation.

From time to time exchanges of prisoners were arranged. In one memorable situation, General Washington refused to exchange healthy Hessian soldier captives for sick and emaciated American soldiers held by the British, as he felt that the Americans would be of no use to the Continental Army, while the Hessians would quickly re-enter the service of the enemy.[3]

On October 28 the *New York Gazette*, now in enemy territory, carried this advertisement, propaganda intended to imply that the currency was useless as money:

The upper works of the Newgate Prison with a guard house on the corner, as it appeared in 1905. During the Revolutionary War the abandoned copper mines deep under the structure were used by the Continental army to imprison the British and their mercenary Hessian soldiers.

The British occupation of New York lasted until the
end of the war. This print shows a man on a flagpole
replacing the British flag with an American one, as the
British fleet departs New York Harbor in November 1783.

Wanted, by a gentleman fond of curiosities, who is shortly going to England, a parcel of Congress bills with which he intends to paper some rooms. Those who wish to make something of their stock in that commodity, shall if they are clean and fit for the purpose, receive at the rate of one guinea per thousand for all they can bring before the expiration of the present month. Inquire of the printer. N.B. It is expected that they will be much lower.

General George Washington (center) with General Artemas Ward (right), an aide-de-camp, and Ward's troops during the Revolutionary War.

ONGOING CURRENCY PROBLEMS

In Philadelphia on December 14, 1776, Major General Israel Putnam reported that General George Washington "to his astonishment has been informed that several of the inhabitants have refused to take the Continental Currency in payment of goods." Washington declared that anyone engaging in this refusal would forfeit their goods and be jailed.[4]

The first issue, authorized by the session of May 10, 1775, held its value fairly well, as did the next several releases. Depreciation began in the spring of 1776 but was so slight that the public was not alarmed.[5] This, of course, was before Washington's army lost New York City and began its long retreat across New Jersey and before the Declaration of Independence was issued. These events settled in the minds of many colonists that what they initially believed to be a short conflict to redress limited political grievances was now going to be a protracted war for independence.

By January 1, 1777, it took the equivalent of $1.05 in paper to buy $1.00 in Spanish-American silver coins, growing to $1.07 in the next month. Contemporary sources vary widely in their estimates of depreciation. A letter from financier Robert Morris to friends in France, dated December 21, 1776, stated that Continental Currency was worth only about 40 percent of what it had been earlier.[6]

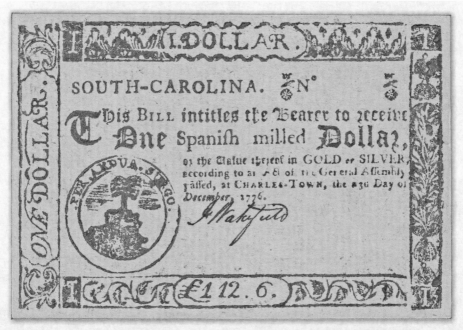

South Carolina paper money from 1777 equal to one Spanish milled dollar.

By January 1778 the value had slipped to the point that $3.25 was required to equal $1 in gold or silver, then $7.42 in January 1779. The last Continental Currency issue was authorized by the session of January 14, 1779, and included the record-high denomination of $80, which was by then needed to make up for the loss in purchasing power of the bills.

After the last emission of Continental Currency in 1779, estimates of the total issue ranged from about $200 million to $360 million, an amount greater than all the gold and silver in the American colonies when the war began. In the meantime some of the states had issued their own paper money, including for soldiers' pay, a subject beyond the purview of the present text.

THE CONTINUING STORY

On December 3, 1777, Congress recommended that the various states enact legislation to require that currency issued by the colonies under the aegis of Great Britain be exchanged for Continental Currency, and that after a period the former would become worthless.

It was further resolved:

> That all bills of credit emitted by Congress ought to pass current in payments, trade, and dealing in these states and shall be deemed in value equal to the Spanish dollar; and it is further recommended to the legislatures of those states to pass laws inflicting forfeitures and other penalties on all who do not sell their lands, houses, goods, &c., for Continental bills as specie value; and that the said legislatures be requested to make the bills of credit issued by Congress a lawful tender in payment of public and private debts, and . . . debts payable in sterling money be discharged with Continental dollars at four shillings and sixpence sterling per dollar (that is to say, at par), and that in discharge of all other debts and contracts, Continental dollars pass at the rate of a Spanish milled dollar.

By that time Continental Currency was trading at a discount. To allow older debts to be paid at par in such bills was tantamount to ruining the saving of many citizens. It remained a crime to state publicly that the bills were worth less than par value in relation to coins! Anyone doing so was subject to imprisonment and confiscation of goods. Quakers who for religious reasons refused to handle money were prosecuted in large numbers.[7] The British in occupied areas paid for goods in silver and gold, resulting in the secret funneling of many agricultural and manufactured products to the enemy.[8]

For new purchases and arrangements there was no problem. The price of goods and services was raised to account for the depreciation of the bills. Citizens did not understand that at all, and many newspaper accounts accused merchants and others of recklessly profiteering! In actuality, they were receiving no more in the net value of payments than before the price inflation of goods occurred.

Most soldiers in the Continental Army continued to receive regular pay in Continental Currency, making it nearly impossible to buy expensive goods outside of the camps.

Continental Currency bills were denominated in "Spanish milled dollars, or the value thereof in gold or silver." In reality the bills could be exchanged for other Continental Currency denominations but not at face value for much else. The federal Treasury was nearly empty. The total amount of silver and gold received in 1778 was just $78,866, and for 1779 the figure was only $73,000.[9] The specie supply had been drained by purchases of military goods from France.

In 1778 and 1779 advertisements offering goods for sale or at auction, payable in Continental Currency, continued to appear. Hardly anything was said

In addition to the hardships of war, including disease and exposure to the elements, soldiers found that their pay lost its buying power as Continental Currency depreciated.

about the great depreciation of the bills, as this would have been viewed as disloyal or treasonous. Instead, the prices of goods and services multiplied in terms of Continental Currency.

On June 3, 1779, Colonel Thomas Fitch, Captain Eliphalet Lockwood, and Samuel C. Silliman were chosen as a committee to gather with citizens at a meeting to be held in Fairfield, Connecticut, "respecting the depreciation of Continental Currency."[10] Presumably, the inflated prices of goods and services were discussed.

At a meeting in Lancaster, Pennsylvania, on June 16, 1779, citizens expressed distress with the high prices of rum, whiskey, molasses, tea, sugar, salt, wheat, flour, and other goods and suggested that if the prices could be lowered, this "should raise the value of our Continental Currency."[11]

The exchange rate inflated to $29.34 in currency for $1 in Spanish silver dollars in January 1780, then to $74.00 in January 1781. In the next month the rate was $75.00, at which time trading in such bills virtually ended in the northern states, with bills being worth about 1/75th of their face value. The bills continue to trade in parts of Virginia and North Carolina for about another year, during which time they depreciated to 1/1000th of face value.

Extensive losses were sustained by anyone who received such money, even at a discount, and held it for any length of time.

As time went on and the financial strength of the Continental Congress became weaker and weaker, the bills depreciated to the point at which they were nearly worthless by 1781. The final accounting of General Washington with the Treasury in Continental Currency was in May of that year. It is relevant to say that without these bills the United States could not have paid its troops and otherwise conducted the Revolution-

Robert Morris.

ary War. Citizens of means paid the price, and more than just a few landed in debtors' prisons (including Robert Morris, who was confined for four years).

A January 5, 1781, bill of sale given to Capt. A. McLane by William Nicholls and paid in Continental Currency shows the dramatic effects of depreciation:

> 1 pair of boots $600
> 6¼ yards of calico $752
> 6 yards of chintz $900
> 4½ yards of moreen $450
> 4 handkerchiefs $400
> 8 yards of quality binding $32
> 1 skein of silk $10
> £$3,144 [equivalent if paid in paper]
> If paid in specie £18, 10s[12]

In the early 1780s Virginia opened a land office to grant warrants for the purchase of 1,000 acres of unsettled land. Certain sums of depreciated Continental Currency were allowed in payment. "The great plenty and little value of this money soon caused the whole country to be located, which was one of the material causes of its rapid population."[13]

Pelatiah Webster in "An Essay on Trade and Finance," Philadelphia, February 10, 1780, summarized the situation:

The people of the states at that time had been worried and fretted, disappointed and put out of humor by so many tender-acts, limitations of prices, and other compulsory methods to force value into piper money, and compel the circulation of it, and by so many vain funding schemes, declarations, and promises, all which issued from Congress, but died under the most zealous efforts to put them into operation and effect, that their patience was all exhausted; I say, these irritations and disappointments had so destroyed the courage and confidence of the people, that they appeared heartless and almost stupid when their attention was called to any new impositions.

Webster in "Remarks on the Resolution of Council of the 2d of May, 1781, for raising the exchange to 175 [paper] Continental dollars for 1 hard," Philadelphia, May 9, 1781, stated this:

It has polluted the equity of our laws, turned them into engines of oppression and wrong, corrupted the justice of our public administrations, destroyed the fortunes of thousands who had the most confidence in it, enervated the trade, husbandry, and manufactures of the country, and went far to destroy the morality of our people. . . .

We have suffered more from this cause than from every other cause or calamity. It has killed more men, pervaded and corrupted the choicest interests of our country more, and done more injustice than even the arms and artifices of the enemy.

REDEMPTION

Although such currency no longer had value in commerce, speculators who hoped that someday the government would redeem it bought quantities at deep discounts, down to 1/1000th of face value or even lower. It is doubtful the new Constitution would have been ratified but for the fact that it promised that the new federal government would honor the debts of the Continental Congress. Wise buyers profited greatly when an act of Congress, passed August 4, 1790, provided that Continental paper money would be received at the Treasury until September 1, 1791, at the new rate of $100 in bills to $1 in gold or silver coins.

One such speculator is said to have been "Lord" Timothy Dexter of Newburyport, Massachusetts, who used his fortune to build a mansion that remains prominent in that town today. Marrying a wealthy widow may have helped as well. The very definition of an eccentric citizen, his activities included conducting

Lord Timothy Dexter.

a mock funeral for himself (by dressing his wife and children in mourning clothes and sending out invitations to townspeople to attend the ceremony; a man was hired to serve as a priest) and publishing a booklet, *A Pickle for the Knowing Ones*, which had a lack of punctuation that could be corrected by readers using extra periods, commas, question marks, and exclamation points placed on a page at the end![14] He called himself "the first in the East, the first in the West, greatest philosopher in the known world." His residence was described by biographer Samuel L. Knapp in 1852:

The house was capacious and well finished, and the out-houses tasteful and commodious. A lovelier spot or a more airy mansion, Lucullus himself could not have wished; and all his ponds would not have furnished a greater variety of excellent fish than the Newburyport market supplied. When Dexter bought this seat everything about it was in fine order; but it was not to the taste of the purchaser.

He raised minarets on the roof of his mansion, surmounted by gilt balls in profusion; and the whole building was painted as finely as a fiddle. One who marked the alteration compared it to a person changing the robes of a peer and, assuming the motley dress of a harlequin; but this made the bumpkins stare, and gave the owner the greatest pleasure. In all the agitations of a vitiated taste, Dexter went on with his *supposed improvements*.

In the garden, which extended several hundreds of feet on the noble high-way, passing in front of it, and was filled with fruit and flowers of indigenous growth, or those imported from Europe, or acclimated from warmer regions, the tasteless owner, in his rage for notoriety, created rows of columns, fifteen feet at least, high, on which to place colossal images carved in wood. Directly in front of the door of the house, on a Roman arch of great beauty and taste, stood General Washington in his military garb. On his left hand was Jefferson; on his right, Adams, uncovered, for he would suffer no one to be on the right of Washington with a hat on.

On the columns in the garden there were figures of Indian chiefs, military generals, philosophers, politicians and statesmen, now and then a goddess of Fame, or Liberty, meretricious enough to be either. . . .

There were upwards of forty of the figures, including four lions, two couchant, and two passant. These were well carved, and attracted more attention from those who had any taste than all the exhibition except the arch, on which stood the three presidents. The lions were open mouthed and fierce as if they had been rampart in heraldic glory.

The Act of May 8, 1791, extended the redemption period to March 7, 1792, after which time all Continental Currency bills were repudiated, the status they retain today.

The depreciation of paper money was long remembered. In later years items of no value were sometimes stated as "Not worth a Continental." This had a lingering effect on later issuance of federal paper money. It was not until 1861 that federal currency again circulated widely. In the meantime, beginning in 1782, state-chartered banks issued their own currency, over 3,000 institutions in all. The first (1791–1811) and second (1816–1836) Bank of the United States also issued paper money.[15]

A view of Timothy Dexter's mansion (also see this book's introduction).

ASPECTS OF COLLECTING

The Continental Congress authorized and issued paper money in 11 different series dated from May 10, 1775, to January 14, 1779. Today all are highly collectible. Considered to be the key issue is the beautiful $20 bill of May 10, 1775, printed on thin French paper with a marbled end, imported under the direction of Benjamin Franklin. As noted, in addition to regular issues, thick rag paper with mica flakes and blue fibers, to deter counterfeiting, was used for all other issues. The bills dated April 11, 1778, are imprinted "York-Town," having been authorized when the Continental Congress was in session in York, Pennsylvania. This particular series was extensively counterfeited, resulting in many being called in and replaced with other bills. As a result the York-Town bills, issued in denominations from $4 to $40, are especially scarce today and highly sought by collectors. As time went on and the bills depreciated in value, lower denominations were dropped from new issues and higher values were added, up to $80.

The typical Continental Currency bill found today will show evidence of circulation, sometimes considerable. The earlier the issue, the more likely it is to have extensive wear. A high-grade, especially desirable bill might be called Extremely Fine or better and should have these characteristics:

This $30 note shows the blue fibers used to deter counterfeiting.

1. The borders should be full, although perhaps closely trimmed (as bills were spaced closely on sheets), with no trimming cutting into the frame or design.

2. The signatures, applied in ink, should all be visible, but not necessarily bold. Some inks, especially those of red hues, faded more than others. Certain certification services *do not* take the clarity of signatures into consideration. Therefore, cherrypicking is needed to be sure signatures are clearly visible.

3. The printing and designs should be clear.

4. The body of the bill should be solid, not easily bendable on a fold or crease. The corners should be fairly sharp, not worn or rounded.

Although a bill exhibiting all of these characteristics is ideal, there is an active market for lower grades, including examples that are trimmed into the borders or have faded signatures or other deficiencies. The tradeoff is that these often sell for much lower prices and that, except for the French-paper $20 of May 10, 1775, a complete collection can be acquired for moderate cost.

Forming a set of Continental Currency paper money at any grade level requires patience and care. Even in lower grades, many of the bills are elusive

This 1778 $30 note has been graded, certified, and set in a Paper Money Guaranty (PMG) slab.

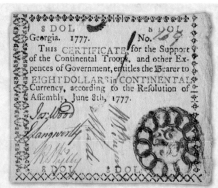

This $20 note from May 1775 has folded edges on the marbled border, as well as creases and other damage to the paper.

This $8 Georgia note from 1777 has a blurred seal on the lower right.

Due to poor trimming, part of the border frame of this $70 note has been cut off.

The full border of this fractional note can be seen.

Clear signatures can be seen on this $4 note from 1778.

Faded signatures left this note with a blank space below the issue date.

and come on the market only at widely separated intervals. A combination of auctions, inquiries to specialist dealers, and attendance at coin shows is the best way to build a collection. Buy carefully, as a bill that is "just right" within a given grade will certainly come along sooner or later. Except for experienced specialists, it is probably best to start by buying only bills graded and certified as genuine by a leading service.

The easiest route is to acquire one bill of each denomination, as this will include each motto and design. An expanded collection might include one of each date and denomination within that date. A collection can be formed by autograph combinations and varieties, of which there are multiples within given dates and denominations. This path is rarely followed by collectors, however.

Illustrated auction catalogs of the past several decades provide a rich source of images—useful for learning about the clarity of printing, border trimming, and related characteristics. Sharply focused Internet images are even better. Contemporary counterfeits (made during the era of the originals) of Continental Currency bills, described and sold as such, are collected by many numismatists and often sell for more than the genuine bills they mimic. The masterwork for historical and other information is Eric P. Newman's *Early Paper Money of America*.

HIDDEN GEMS OF INTEREST

Studying and collecting the signatures of members of the Continental Congress is an interesting pursuit. So is researching to connect these bills to the history of the Revolutionary War. Only one signer of the Declaration of Independence also inked his name on Continental Currency: James Wilson of Pennsylvania.

Some border engravings are attributed to David Rittenhouse, who years later in 1792 was appointed as first director of the U.S. Mint. No listing of Rittenhouse borders has ever been published.

David Rittenhouse.

Some border engravings are attributed to David Rittenhouse, who years later in 1792 was appointed as first director of the U.S. Mint. No listing of Rittenhouse borders has ever been published.

TRIBVLATIO
DITAT.

Si tritura absit, paleis sunt abdita grana:
Nos crux mundanis separat à paleis.

Y 2

Title page and an image
from the Camerarius study.

JOACHIMI CAMERARII
MEDICI. V. CL.

SYMBOLORVM
ET
EMBLEMATVM
CENTVRIÆ TRES.

I.   Ex herbis & stirpibus.
II. Ex animalibus quadrupedibus.
III. Ex volatilibus & insectis.

Editio secunda, auctior & accuratior.

ACCESSIT NOVITER
CENTVRIA
IV. Ex aquatilibus & reptilibus.

CVM FIGVRIS ÆNEIS.

TYPIS VOEGELINIANIS.

ANNO M.DC.V.

2

Emblems and Mottoes, Production and Distribution

EMBLEMS AND MOTTOES

The emblems and mottoes used on Continental Currency are for the most part not original. Some were used on colonial bills. They were selected by Benjamin Franklin, who may have been inspired by a 1605 book of mottoes by Dr. Joachim Camerarius, *Symbolorum et Emblematum Centuriæ Tres*, which contained no images copied for use on the bills, although *Tribulatio Ditat* ("Troubles make us stronger") contained some elements of the same motto illustrated on currency.

Descriptions with explanations were published by Wayte Raymond in his *Standard Catalogue* in the 1930s.

Relatively few of the Latin inscriptions were understandable by the average American citizen at the time.

Pennsylvania Magazine, December 1775, gave descriptions of the emblems on the bills issued up to that date, the $1 to $8, $20, and $30 (quoted below).

Benjamin Franklin was a guiding hand in selecting many of the emblems and mottoes that appeared on Continental Currency.

$1/6, $1/3, $1/2, and $2/3 • FUGIO MIND YOUR BUSINESS • *Translation of "FUGIO"*: I fly. *Meaning*: Time flies, therefore tend to your business. *Motif*: Sundial. This motif was also used on the 1776 Continental dollar coin and the 1787 Fugio copper.

$1 • DEPRESSA RESURGIT • *Translation*: Though pressed down it rises again. *Motif*: The allegory is to the subjugation of the colonies by England. Motif of a thistle with a heavy beard on its blossom.

Pennsylvania Magazine, December 1775:

> On the $1 bill, we have the plant acanthus, sprouting on all sides, under a weight placed upon it, with the motto, DEPRESSA RESURGIT— "though oppressed it rises."—The ancients tell us that the sight of such an

accidental circumstance, gave the first hint to an architect in forming the beautiful capital of the Corinthian column. This, perhaps, was intended to encourage us by representing that our present oppressions will not destroy us, but that they may, by increasing our industry, and forcing it into new courses, increase the prosperity on the base of liberty, and the well-proportioned pillar of property, elevated for a pleasing spectacle to all connoisseurs, who can taste and delight in the architecture of human happiness.

$2 • TRIBULATIO DITAT • *Translation*: Affliction enriches; troubles make us stronger. *Motif*: Hand holding tool, a flail. The allegory is that the American people, at war with England, are undergoing travails, but this can be beneficial in a way.

Pennsylvania Magazine, December 1775:

> On the $2 bill is a figure of a hand and flail, over sheaves of wheat, with the motto, TRIBULATIO DITAT—"threshing improves it;" (which we find printed on another of the bills) may perhaps be intended to admonish us, that though at present we are under the flail its blows, how hard so ever, will be rather advantageous than hurtful to us; for they will bring forth every grain of genius and merit in arts, manufactures war and council, that are now concealed in the husk, and then the breath of a breeze will be sufficient to separate from us all the chaff, or toryism.
>
> Tribula, too, in our English sense of the word, improves the mind, it makes us humbler and tends to make us wiser. And threshing, in one of its senses,

that of beating, often improves those that are threshed. Many an unwarlike nation have been beaten into heroes, by troublesome warlike neighbors; and the continuance of a war, though it lessen the numbers of a people, often increases its strength by the increased discipline and consequent courage of the number remaining. Thus England, after the civil war, in which her people threshed one another, became more formidable to her neighbors. The public distress, too, that arises from war, by increasing frugality and industry, often gives rise to habits that remain after the war is over, and thereby naturally enriches those on whom it has enforced, those enriching virtues.

$3 • EXITUS IN DUBIO EST • *Translation*: The end is in doubt. *Motif*: Bird of prey fighting. The lower bird on its back. The allegory is to the conflict between the United States and England.

Pennsylvania Magazine, December 1775:

> On the $3 bill is drawn an eagle on the wing pouncing upon a crane, who turns upon his back and receives the eagle on the point of his long bill, which pierces the eagle's breast; with this motto, EXITUS IN DUBIO EST—"the event is uncertain." The eagle, I suppose, represents Great Britain, the crane America: this device offers an admonition to each of the contending parties. To the crane, not to depend too much upon the success of its endeavors to avoid the contest (by petition, negotiation, &c.) but to prepare for using the means God and nature hath given it; and to the eagle, not to presume on its superior and strength, since a weaker bird may wound it mortally.

$4 • AUT MORS AUT VITA DECORA • *Translation*: Either death or an honorable life. *Motif*: A running boar is about to impale itself on a spear tip. *Pennsylvania Magazine*, December 1775:

> On the $4 bill is impressed, a wild boar of the forest, rushing on the spear of the hunter, with this motto, AUT MORS AUT VITA DECORA; which may be translated—"death or liberty." The wild boar is an animal of great strength and courage, armed with long and sharp tusks, which he well knows how to use in his own defense. His is inoffensive while suffered to enjoy his freedom, but when roused and wounded by the hunter, often turns and makes him pay dearly for his temerity.

$5 • SUSTINE VEL ABSTINE • *Translation*: Sustain or abstain. *Motif*: Hand caressing growing bush. Either help nourish a movement, such as the independence of America, or abstain.

Pennsylvania Magazine, December 1775:

> On the $5 bill, we have a thorny bush, which a hand seems attempting to eradicate; the hand appears to bleed, as pricked by the spines. The motto is SUBSTINE [*sic*] VEL ABSTINE; which may be rendered "bear with me, or let me alone," or thus, "either support or leave me." The bush I suppose to mean America, and the bleeding hand Britain. Would to God that bleeding were stopt; the wounds of that hand healed, and its future operation directed by wisdom and equity; so shall the hawthorn flourish and form an hedge around it, annoying with her thorns only its invading enemies.

$6 • **PERSEVERANDO** • *Translation*: By persevering. *Motif*: Beaver gnawing a tree (England, although a *palm* is shown). By persevering the beaver slowly eats away at the tree trunk until it collapses.

Pennsylvania Magazine, December 1775:

> The $6 bill has the figure of a beaver, gnawing a large tree, with this motto, PERSEVERANDO—"by perseverance." I apprehend the great tree may be intended to represent the enormous power Britain has assumed over us and endeavors to enforce by arms, of taxing at pleasure, and binding us in all cases whatsoever, or the exorbitant profits she makes by monopolizing our commerce.—Then the beaver, which is known to be able, by assiduous and steady working, to fell large trees, may signify America; which, by perseverance in her present measures, will probably reduce that power within proper bounds, and, by establishing the most necessary manufactures among ourselves, abolish the British monopoly.

$7 • **SERENABIT** • *Translation*: It will clear up. *Motif*: Storm clouds and rain over a landscape. The allegory is that war, now in progress, will eventually end.

Pennsylvania Magazine, December 1775:

> The $7 bill has for its device, a storm descending from a black heavy cloud, with the motto, SERENABIT—"it will clear up." This seems designed to encourage the dejected, who may be too sensible of present inconveniences, and fear their continuance. It reminds them, agreeably to the adage, that after a storm comes a calm. . . .

$8 • MAJORA MINORIBUS CONSONANT • *Translation*: The greater ones sound in harmony with the smaller. *Motif*: An ornate harp with thirteen strings. The allegory is that all states, large and small, are in harmony with each other.

Pennsylvania Magazine, December 1775:

> On the $8 denomination of the bills, there is the figure of a harp, with this motto, MAJORA MINORIBUS CONSONANT; literally—"the greater and smaller ones sound together." As the harp is an instrument composed of great and small strings, included in a strong frame, and also so tuned as to agree in concord with each other, I conceive that the frame may be intended to represent our new government by a continental congress, and the strings of different lengths and substance, either the several colonies of different weights and force, or the various ranks of people in all of them, who are now united by that government in the most perfect harmony.

$20 • VI CONCITATÆ • *Translation*: Having been bestirred. *Motif*: The face of a sun emits rays and fire on the landscape below. Meaning: A nation has been awakened. French paper (May 10, 1775) and later regular paper issues.

Pennsylvania Magazine, December 1775:

> On the $20 bill, there is stamped the representation of a tempestuous sea; a face with swollen cheeks, wrapt up in a black cloud, appearing to blow violently on the waters, the waves high, and all rolling one way. The motto, VI CONCITATE [*sic*]; which may be rendered—"raised by force." From the remotest antiquity, in figurative language, great waters have signified the people, and waves an insurrection. The people of themselves are sup-posed as naturally inclined to be still, the waters to remain level and quiet. Their rising here appears not be from any internal cause, but from an external power, expressing by the head Eolus, god of the winds, (or Boreas, the North wind, as usually the most violent) acting furiously upon them. The black cloud perhaps, designs the British parliament, and the waves the colonies. Their rolling all in one direction, shows, that the very force used against them, has produced their unanimity.
>
> On the reverse of this bill, we have a smooth sea, the sails of ships on that sea hanging loose, show a perfect calm, the sun shining fully, denotes a clear sky. The motto is CESSANTES VENTO CON QUIECEMUS—"the wind ceasing, we shall be quiet." Supposing my explanation of the preceding device to be right, this will import, that when those violent acts of power which have roused the colonies are repealed, they will return to

their former tranquility. Britain seems thus charged with being the sole cause of the present civil war, at the same time that the only mode of putting an end to it, is thus plainly pointed out to her.

$30 • SI RECTE FACIES • *Translation*: If thou shall do well. *Motif*: Laurel wreath of pedestal. The allegory is those that do well are recognized.

Pennsylvania Magazine, December 1775:

> The last, the $30 bill, has a wreath of laurel on a marble monument or altar: the motto, SI RECTE FACIES—"if you act rightly." This seems intended as an encouragement to a brave and steady conduct in defense of our Liberties, as it promises to crown with honor, by the laurel wreath, those who persevere to the end in well-doing; and with a long duration of that honor, expressed by the monument of marble.
>
> A learned friend of mine thinks this device more particularly addressed to the *Congress*. He says that the ancients composed for their heroes a wreath of laurel, oak and olive twigs interwoven. . . .
>
> Of laurel, as that tree was dedicated to Apollo, and understood to signify knowledge and prudence; of oak, as pertaining to Jupiter, and expressing fortitude; of olive, as the tree of Pallas, and as a symbol of peace. The whole to show, that those who are entrusted to conduct the great affairs of mankind, should act prudently and firmly, retaining, above all, upon an altar, to admonish the hero who is to be crowned with it, that true glory is founded on, and proceeds from piety. My friend, therefore, thinks the

present device might intend a wreath of that composite kind, though, from the smallness of the work, the engraver could not mark distinctly the differing leaves. And he is rather confirmed in his opinion that this is designed as an admonition to the Congress, when he considers the passage in Horace, from whence the motto is taken—

Rex eris, aium,

Si recte facies. . . .

Not the king's parliament, who act wrong, but the people's congress, if it acts right, shall govern America.

$35 • HINC OPES • *Translation*: Hence our wealth. *Motif*: Symbolic of agriculture being the strength of America.

$40 • CONFEDERATION • *Motif*: All Seeing Eye with thirteen stars. Represents the confederation of the states.

$45 • SIC FLORET RESPUBLICA • *Translation*: Thus flourishes the Republic. *Motif*: Two skep-type beehives under cover, with bees flying nearby. The allegory is that industry and activity sustain the republic.

$50 • PERENNIS • *Translation*: Everlasting. *Motif*: Illustration of a step pyramid, representing durability.

$55 • POST NUBILA PHŒBUS • *Translation*: After the clouds comes the sun. *Motif*: Landscape with clouds on the left departing and with the sun, on the right, bathing trees and ground in light. The allegory is that after the war there will be peace.

$60 • DEUS REGNAT EXULTET TERRA • *Translation*: The Lord reigneth, let the world rejoice. *Motif*: Illustration of a globe in space, representing the earth.

$65 • FIAT JUSTITIA • *Translation*: Let justice be done. *Motif*: A hand holding scales of justice. In the conflict, justice will eventually prevail.

$70 • VIM PROCELLARUM QUADRENNIUM SUSTINUIT • *Translation*: For four years it has sustained the force of the gales. *Motif*: A leafy tree flourishing on a hillside, apparently with sunny skies. The allegory is that after being tossed by wind and rain (four years of war) the tree at last flourishes.

$80 • ET IN SECULA SECULORUM FLORESCEBIT • *Translation*: It will flourish forever and ever. *Motif*: Sturdy oak tree on solid ground. The allegory is that America, the oak, will be ever enduring.

Production and Distribution

Continental Currency was printed by Hall & Sellers (William Hall and William Sellers), located on Market Street, Philadelphia, the successor to a business founded by Benjamin Franklin. The firm also produced bills for some of the colonies. Bills were printed in sheets with multiple denominations on each.

Forms were made that included engraved metal vignettes and borders produced by David Rittenhouse and possibly by James Smither. None are signed. No specific attributions have ever been published. This included emblems enclosed in circles and rectangular elements for each of the four borders. These were replaced from time to time when they became worn. Thus, a typical emblem used in many issues was made in multiple minor varieties, each with topological differences.[1] Letters and numerals were hand-set in individual type. All paper was made by Willcox & Company at Ivy Mills in Delaware County near Philadelphia, with the sole exception of the aforementioned $20 bills of the May 10, 1775, issue printed on paper imported from France.[2] Each sheet was thick—the British called the bills "the pasteboard money of the rebels"—and contained mica flakes as a deterrent to counterfeiting.

On most issues "nature printing" was used on the back. This usually consisted of a plate made from a casting of one or several leaves taken from plants and trees.[3] It was thought that counterfeiters would not be able to duplicate

The southeast corner of Third and Market streets in Philadelphia.

the veins and other characteristics. The process was invented by Benjamin Franklin and was also used on bills issued by Delaware, Maryland, New Jersey, and Pennsylvania.[4] The design elements of the leaf impressions proved to be surprisingly durable and did not deteriorate during the printing of large quantities of bills, usually extending through several series.

The paper was slightly dampened prior to printing on a hand-operated lever press. The metal type and ornaments pressed into the surface created a slightly rough surface—a contrast to certain colonial and later state-chartered bank bills printed from copper or steel plates.

The bills were then signed and cut apart, often roughly with irregular edges. Bills of $1 or less were given one signature. Higher denominations were signed by two appointed individuals (see appendix A), one signing in red ink and the other in brown or black. Serial numbers were inked in by hand.

The bills were paid out by the Treasury for goods and services, including the wages of soldiers. Continental Currency began to depreciate almost immediately and was worth pennies on the dollar by the time of the last issue in 1779. Soldiers' pay, although adjusted from time to time, was always short of the amount needed to buy items desired. Government purchases for goods and services cost ever-increasing amounts as prices were raised across the board by sellers.

Face of a Continental Currency bill with the five inserted plate elements outlined in green.

Back of a bill with the nature printing plate (outlined in green) inserted within the frame plate.

A view of Independence Hall in Philadelphia, by William Birch.

3
Continental Bills Issued

The notes dated May 10, 1775, were issued with high hopes. The patriotic motifs reflected the spirit of independence of the day and were intended to assure a wide circulation. At the outset, Continental notes traded at close to the value of silver coins, but that proved to be short-lived. The figures of quantities issued are from official reports, but it is likely that actual circulation was lower.

The 2009 prices in this chapter are from the *Whitman Encyclopedia of U.S. Paper Money* (2009), and the 2020 prices are provided by Valuations Editor Bruce Hagen.

May 10, 1775
(session)
Authorized amount: $3,000,000
Imprinted Philadelphia

Although these were authorized on May 10, the first bills did not enter circulation until August as many of the appointed signers failed to do their duty and, in any event, the process was very slow.[1] Other bills were paid out as they were signed in ensuing weeks. They were widely accepted at face value and circulated alongside various bills issued by the colonies.

KNOWN SIGNERS OF THE MAY 10, 1775, BILLS

Thomas Barclay; Thomas Barton Jr.; John Bayard (member of the Continental Congress); Andrew Bunner; Daniel Clymer; Thomas Coombe; William Craig; Judah Foulke; Isaac Hazlehurst; William Jackson; Jones, Robert Strettle; Frederick Kuhl; Thomas Laurence (Lawrence); Ellis Lewis; Mordecai Lewis; John Mease; Samuel Meredith (member of the Continental Congress); George Mifflin; James Milligan; Anthony Morris Jr.; John Maxwell Nesbit (Nesbitt); Luke Morris; Samuel Morris; John Purviance; Robert Roberts Jr.; John Shee; Joseph Sims Jr.; Jonathan Bayard Smith (member of the Continental Congress); Robert Tuckniss. *See appendix A for more information.*

Whitman-8501 • $1 • 49,000 printed. Nature printing: One ragweed leaf and two willow leaves.[2]

Signed by
Thomas Coombe and Ellis Lewis.

	VG-8	F-12	VF-20	EF-40	AU-50	Unc-63	Unc-65
2009	$100	$175	$300	$450	$650	$1,200	$1,750
2020	$200	$250	$400	$2,000	$4,000		

Values for notes above $100 are for certified (professionally graded) pieces.

W-8502 • $2 • 49,000 printed. Nature printing: One raspberry leaf and two filbert leaves.

Signed by
Anthony Morris Jr. and Frederick Kuhl.

	VG-8	F-12	VF-20	EF-40	AU-50	Unc-63	Unc-65
2009	$75	$125	$200	$300	$450	$1,000	$2,000
2020	$125	$175	$250	$500	$2,000	$3,500	

Values for notes above $100 are for certified (professionally graded) pieces.

W-8503 • $3 • 49,000 printed. Nature printing: elm leaf section and wings from a maple seed.[3]

**Signed by
Anthony Morris Jr. and Frederick Kuhl.**

	VG-8	F-12	VF-20	EF-40	AU-50	Unc-63	Unc-65
2009	$75	$125	$200	$300	$450	$1,000	$2,000
2020	$100	$150	$200	$400	$750	$2,000	$5,000

Values for notes above $100 are for certified (professionally graded) pieces.

W-8504 • **$4** • 49,000 printed. Nature printing: Sections of wings from a maple seed.[4]

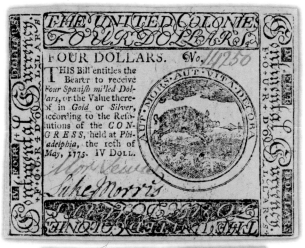

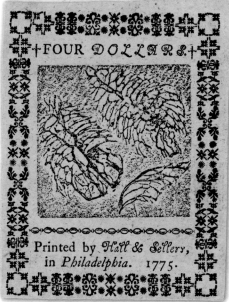

**Signed by
Mordecai Lewis and Luke Morris.**

	VG-8	F-12	VF-20	EF-40	AU-50	Unc-63	Unc-65
2009	$75	$125	$200	$300	$450	$1,000	$2,000
2020	$100	$150	$200	$400	$750	$2,000	$5,000

Values for notes above $100 are for certified (professionally graded) pieces.

W-8505 • **$5** • 49,000 printed. Nature printing: Betony and sage leaves.

Signed by
Isaac Hazlehurst and Judah Foulke.

	VG-8	F-12	VF-20	EF-40	AU-50	Unc-63	Unc-65
2009	$75	$125	$200	$300	$450	$1,000	$2,000
2020	$100	$150	$200	$400	$750	$2,000	$5,000

Values for notes above $100 are for certified (professionally graded) pieces.

W-8506 • **$6** • 49,000 printed. Nature printing: Prominent buttercup leaf.

Signed by
Samuel Morris and Thomas Barton Jr.

	VG-8	F-12	VF-20	EF-40	AU-50	Unc-63	Unc-65
2009	$75	$125	$200	$300	$450	$1,000	$2,000
2020	$100	$150	$200	$400	$750	$2,000	$5,000

Values for notes above $100 are for certified (professionally graded) pieces.

W-8507 • **$7** • 49,000 printed. Nature printing: Prominent buttercup leaf differently oriented.

**Signed by
James Milligan and James Read.**

	VG-8	F-12	VF-20	EF-40	AU-50	Unc-63	Unc-65
2009	$75	$125	$200	$300	$450	$1,000	$2,000
2020	$100	$150	$200	$400	$750	$2,000	$5,000

Values for notes above $100 are for certified (professionally graded) pieces.

W-8508 • $8 • 49,000 printed. Nature printing: Prominent buttercup leaf and two smaller leaves.

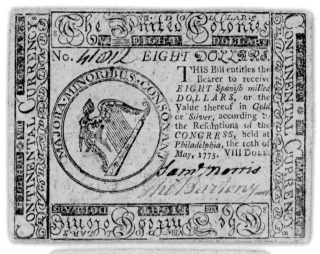

Signed by
Samuel Morris and Thomas Barton Jr.

	VG-8	F-12	VF-20	EF-40	AU-50	Unc-63	Unc-65
2009	$75	$125	$200	$300	$450	$1,000	$2,000
2020	$100	$150	$200	$400	$750	$2,000	$5,000

Values for notes above $100 are for certified (professionally graded) pieces.

W-8509 • **$20** • 11,800 printed. Special French paper issue with marbled left side end on the face of the bill. Back with sun over sea and two ships. These were printed individually from one pair of plates, not in sheets. Most are carefully trimmed.

Signed by
William Craig and John Bayard.

	VG-8	F-12	VF-20	EF-40	AU-50
2009	$800	$2,000	$4,000	$8,000	$12,000
2020	$5,000	$7,500	$20,000	$45,000	$75,000

Values for notes above $100 are for certified (professionally graded) pieces.

W-8510 • $30 • 33,333 printed. Sun over sea with two ships.

Signed by
Samuel Morris and Thomas Barton Jr.

	VG-8	F-12	VF-20	EF-40	AU-50	Unc-63	Unc-65
2009	$100	$175	$400	$500	$700	$1,200	$2,500
2020	$150	$250	$350	$600	$900	$3,000	

Values for notes above $100 are for certified (professionally graded) pieces.

November 29, 1775

(*resolution*, as are the following)
Authorized amount: $3,000,000 plus an additional $10,000
Imprinted Philadelphia

Bills of this date are serially numbered in red ink, to differentiate them at a glance from the preceding. The denominations have been moved to beneath the emblems. Sheets on blue paper were made for the detection of counterfeits, which had become a problem by this time.

Known Signers of the November 29, 1775, Bills

Thomas Barclay; Cornelius Barnes; Phineas Bond; Andrew Bunner; Samuel Caldwell; George Campbell; Matthew Clarkson (member of the Continental Congress); Daniel Clymer; Stephen Collins; Thomas Coombe; William Crispin; Joel Evans; Benjamin Fuller; Nicholas Garrison; Isaac Hazlehurst; Isaac Howell; J. Kuhl; Mordecai Lewis; John Mease; Anthony Morris Jr.; Samuel C. Morris; Thomas Morris; John Ord; Joseph Parker; John Purviance; Robert Roberts Jr.; John Shee; Jonathan Bayard Smith (member of the Continental Congress); Thomas Smith; Robert Tuckniss; Joseph Watkins Jr.; William Webb; James Wharton. *See appendix A for more information.*

W-8511 • **$1** • 83,611 printed. Nature printing: One ragweed leaf and two willow leaves.

**Signed by
Thomas Coombe and Phineas Bond.**

	VG-8	F-12	VF-20	EF-40	AU-50	Unc-63	Unc-65
2009	$80	$125	$200	$300	$450	$950	$1,750
2020	$200	$300	$400	$750	$1,250	$3,500	$5,000

Values for notes above $100 are for certified (professionally graded) pieces.

W-8512 • $2 • 83,611 printed. Nature printing: One raspberry leaf and two filbert leaves.

Signed by
Thomas Coombe and James Read.

	VG-8	F-12	VF-20	EF-40	AU-50	Unc-63	Unc-65
2009	$80	$125	$200	$300	$450	$950	$1,750
2020	$175	$250	$300	$600	$1,000	$2,500	$4,000

Values for notes above $100 are for certified (professionally graded) pieces.

W-8513 • **$3** • 83,611 printed. Nature printing: Elm leaf section and wings from a maple seed.

Signed by
Thomas Coombe and Phineas Bond.

	VG-8	F-12	VF-20	EF-40	AU-50	Unc-63	Unc-65
2009	$80	$125	$200	$300	$450	$950	$1,750
2020	$125	$150	$200	$400	$750	$2,000	$4,000

Values for notes above $100 are for certified (professionally graded) pieces.

W-8514 • **$4** • 83,611 printed. Nature printing: Sections of wings from a maple seed.

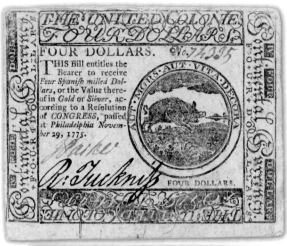

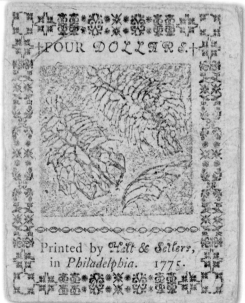

Signed by
Joseph Parker and Robert Tuckniss.

	VG-8	F-12	VF-20	EF-40	AU-50	Unc-63	Unc-65
2009	$80	$125	$200	$300	$450	$950	$1,750
2020	$125	$150	$200	$400	$750	$2,000	$4,000

Values for notes above $100 are for certified (professionally graded) pieces.

W-8515 • $5 • 83,611 printed. Nature printing: Betony and sage leaves.

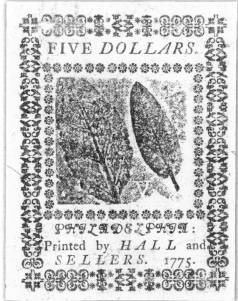

**Signed by
Jonathan Bayard Smith and William Crispin.**

	VG-8	F-12	VF-20	EF-40	AU-50	Unc-63	Unc-65
2009	$80	$125	$200	$300	$450	$950	$1,750
2020	$125	$150	$200	$400	$750	$2,000	$4,000

Values for notes above $100 are for certified (professionally graded) pieces.

W-8516 • $6 • 83,611 printed. Nature printing: Prominent buttercup leaf.

Signed by
J. Kuhl and Anthony Morris Jr.

	VG-8	F-12	VF-20	EF-40	AU-50	Unc-63	Unc-65
2009	$80	$125	$200	$300	$450	$950	$1,750
2020	$125	$150	$200	$400	$750	$2,000	$4,000

Values for notes above $100 are for certified (professionally graded) pieces.

W-8517 • **$7** • 83,611 printed. Nature printing: Prominent buttercup leaf, differently oriented.

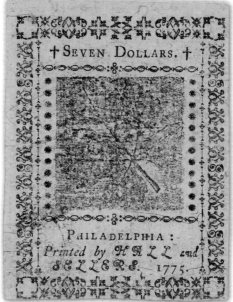

Signed by
Isaac Howell and Robert Roberts Jr.

	VG-8	F-12	VF-20	EF-40	AU-50	Unc-63	Unc-65
2009	$80	$125	$200	$300	$450	$950	$1,750
2020	$125	$150	$200	$400	$750	$2,000	$4,000

Values for notes above $100 are for certified (professionally graded) pieces.

W-8518 • **$8** • 83,611 printed. Nature printing: Prominent buttercup leaf and two smaller leaves.

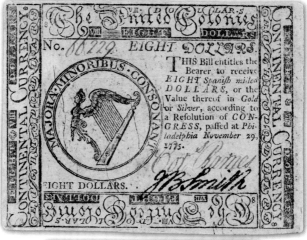

Signed by
Cornelius Barnes and Jonathan Bayard Smith.

	VG-8	F-12	VF-20	EF-40	AU-50	Unc-63	Unc-65
2009	$80	$125	$200	$300	$450	$950	$1,750
2020	$125	$150	$200	$400	$750	$2,000	$4,000

Values for notes above $100 are for certified (professionally graded) pieces.

February 17, 1776

Authorized amount: $4,000,000, including $1,000,000 in fractional bills

The fractional bills, issued only in this series, each have the sundial / linked rings design similar to that used on the 1776 Continental dollar and later adapted for the 1787 Fugio copper cent. In the $1/6 CURRENCEY is a misspelling. Fractional bills bear one signature instead of the two used on larger denominations.

The borders of these were engraved by Elisha Gallaudet (per Newman). The supply of fractional bills was sufficient that they continued to be signed and issued throughout the year, including during the distribution of the next two issues.

Known Signers of the February 17, 1776, Bills

James Ash; Cornelius Barnes; John (Joshua) Barney; Theodore Barrel; Phineas Bond; John Boyd; Benjamin Brannan; Clement Brooks (Brook, Brooke); Joseph Bullock; George Campbell; Daniel Carroll; Matthew Clarkson (member of the Continental Congress); Daniel Clymer; Samuel Stringer Coale; W. Coale; William Coats; Thomas Coombe; Hercules Courtenay (Courtney); Richard Cromwell; Thomas Donellan; William Douglass; David Duncan; Robert Evans; James Ewing; Joseph Gaither; Nicholas Garrison; George Gray Jr.; G. Grier; Isaac Hazlehurst; Robert Hazlehurst; Josiah Hewes; Samuel Hillegas; John Howard; Isaac Howell; Adam Hubley; Benjamin Jacobs; Horatio Johnson; Rinaldo Johnson; John Kaighn; John (James) Kelso; Philip Kinsey; Frederick Kuhl; Peter Kurtz; Thomas Leech; Benjamin Levy; C. Lewis; Mordecai Lewis; William Lux; Zachariah Maccubin (Mackubin); Jacob (Samuel) Massey; William Masters; R. McAlester; John Mease; James Milligan; Anthony Morris Jr.; Samuel C. Morris; Thomas Morris; F. Muir; John Ord; Joseph Parker; C. Parr; Isaac Pearson; John Philpot; John Purviance; William Ramsey (Ramsay); Joseph Redman; Robert A. Roberts; J. Rothrock; John Sellers; Nathan Sellers; Samuel Sellers; David Shaffer (Shaffer, Schaffer) Jr.; John Shaw Jr.; Walter Shee; Jonathan Bayard Smith (member of the Continental Congress); Thomas Smith; William Spear; Peter Stretch; John Taylor; John Thomson; Tench Tilghman; Robert Tuckniss; Andrew Tybout; James Walker; Joseph Watkins Jr.; William Webb; George Welch; Israel Whelen; John Williams (member of the Continental Congress). *See appendix A for more information.*

W-8519 • $1/6 • 600,000 printed. Circle of rings with abbreviated state names; AMERICAN CONGRESS / WE ARE ONE within sunburst at center.

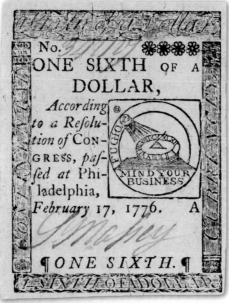

**Signed by
Jacob (Samuel) Massey.**

	VG-8	F-12	VF-20	EF-40	AU-50	Unc-63	Unc-65
2009	$100	$200	$350	$550	$850	$1,800	$3,000
2020	$125	$200	$300	$1,000	$2,000	$4,500	$8,500

Values for notes above $100 are for certified (professionally graded) pieces.

W-8520 • $1/3 • 600,000 printed. Circle of rings with abbreviated state names; AMERICAN CONGRESS / WE ARE ONE within sunburst at center.

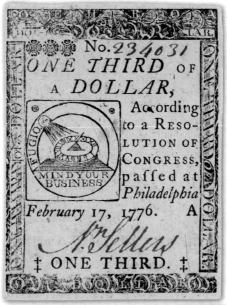

**Signed by
Nathan Sellers.**

	VG-8	F-12	VF-20	EF-40	AU-50	Unc-63	Unc-65
2009	$100	$200	$350	$550	$850	$1,800	$3,000
2020	$125	$200	$250	$750	$1,500	$4,000	$7,500

Values for notes above $100 are for certified (professionally graded) pieces.

W-8521 • $1/2 • 600,000 printed. Circle of rings with abbreviated state names; AMERICAN CONGRESS / WE ARE ONE within sunburst at center.

Signed by
Joseph Redman.

	VG-8	F-12	VF-20	EF-40	AU-50	Unc-63	Unc-65
2009	$100	$200	$350	$550	$850	$1,800	$3,000
2020	$125	$200	$250	$750	$1,500	$4,000	$7,500

Values for notes above $100 are for certified (professionally graded) pieces.

W-8522 • $2/3 • 600,000 printed. Circle of rings with abbreviated state names; AMERICAN CONGRESS / WE ARE ONE within sunburst at center.

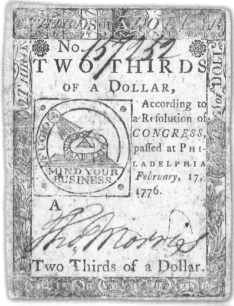

**Signed by
Thomas Morris.**

	VG-8	F-12	VF-20	EF-40	AU-50	Unc-63	Unc-65
2009	$100	$200	$350	$550	$850	$1,800	$3,000
2020	$125	$200	$250	$750	$1,500	$4,000	$7,500

Values for notes above $100 are for certified (professionally graded) pieces.

W-8523 • $1 • 130,436 printed. Nature printing: One ragweed leaf and two willow leaves.

Signed by
Andrew Tybout and Jonas Hewes.

	VG-8	F-12	VF-20	EF-40	AU-50	Unc-63	Unc-65
2009	$90	$125	$225	$375	$450	$1,000	$1,950
2020	$125	$150	$250	$500	$750	$3,000	$4,500

Values for notes above $100 are for certified (professionally graded) pieces.

W-8524 • $2 • 130,437 printed. Nature printing: One raspberry leaf and two filbert leaves.

Signed by
John Ord and Matthew Clarkson.

	VG-8	F-12	VF-20	EF-40	AU-50	Unc-63	Unc-65
2009	$90	$125	$225	$375	$450	$1,000	$1,950
2020	$100	$125	$200	$400	$600	$2,000	$3,500

Values for notes above $100 are for certified (professionally graded) pieces.

W-8525 • $3 • 130,436 printed. Nature printing: elm leaf section and wings from a maple seed.

**Signed by
Walter Shee and Robert Hazlehurst.**

	VG-8	F-12	VF-20	EF-40	AU-50	Unc-63	Unc-65
2009	$90	$125	$225	$375	$450	$1,000	$1,950
2020	$100	$125	$150	$350	$500	$1,500	$3,000

Values for notes above $100 are for certified (professionally graded) pieces.

W-8526 • $4 • 130,435 printed. Nature printing: sections of wings from a maple seed.

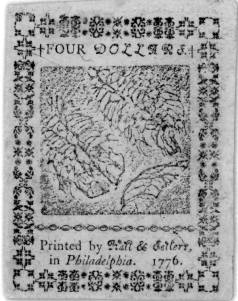

**Signed by
John Howard and Peter Stretch.**

	VG-8	F-12	VF-20	EF-40	AU-50	Unc-63	Unc-65
2009	$90	$125	$225	$375	$450	$1,000	$1,950
2020	$100	$125	$150	$350	$500	$1,500	$3,000

Values for notes above $100 are for certified (professionally graded) pieces.

W-8527 • $5 • 65,217 printed. Nature printing: Betony and sage leaves.

Signed by
William Webb and Robert Hazlehurst.

	VG-8	F-12	VF-20	EF-40	AU-50	Unc-63	Unc-65
2009	$90	$125	$225	$375	$450	$1,000	$1,950
2020	$100	$125	$150	$350	$500	$1,500	$3,000

Values for notes above $100 are for certified (professionally graded) pieces.

W-8528 • $6 • 65,217 printed. Nature printing: Prominent buttercup leaf.

Signed by
William Coats and John Williams.

	VG-8	F-12	VF-20	EF-40	AU-50	Unc-63	Unc-65
2009	$90	$125	$225	$375	$450	$1,000	$1,950
2020	$100	$125	$150	$350	$500	$1,500	$3,000

Values for notes above $100 are for certified (professionally graded) pieces.

W-8529 • $7 • 65,217 printed. Nature printing: Prominent buttercup leaf, differently oriented.

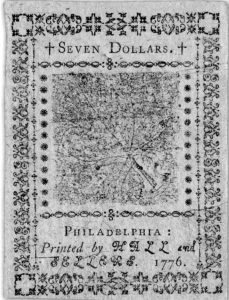

Signed by
William Coats and John Williams.

	VG-8	F-12	VF-20	EF-40	AU-50	Unc-63	Unc-65
2009	$90	$125	$225	$375	$450	$1,000	$1,950
2020	$100	$125	$150	$350	$500	$1,500	$3,000

Values for notes above $100 are for certified (professionally graded) pieces.

W-8530 • $8 • 65,217 printed. Nature printing: Prominent buttercup leaf and two smaller leaves.

Signed by
William Coats and John Williams.

	VG-8	F-12	VF-20	EF-40	AU-50	Unc-63	Unc-65
2009	$90	$125	$225	$375	$450	$1,000	$1,950
2020	$100	$125	$150	$350	$500	$1,500	$3,000

Values for notes above $100 are for certified (professionally graded) pieces.

May 9, 1776

Authorized amount: $5,000,000
Imprinted Philadelphia

Sheets of bills on blue paper were printed for counterfeit detection.

KNOWN SIGNERS OF THE MAY 9, 1776, BILLS

James Ash; Cornelius Barnes; Phineas Bond; Benjamin Brannan; George Campbell; Matthew Clarkson (member of the Continental Congress); Daniel Clymer; W. Coale; Thomas Coombe; Joel Evans; Robert Evans; Nicholas Garrison; George Gray Jr.; Robert Hazlehurst; Josiah Hewes; Samuel Hillegas; John Howard; Isaac Howell; Adam Hubley; James Johnston; Philip Kinsey; Frederick Kuhl; Thomas Leech; Mordecai Lewis; Jacob (Samuel) Massey; William Masters; Anthony Morris Jr.; Samuel C. Morris; Thomas Morris; F. Muir; John Ord; Joseph Parker; Isaac Pearson; Joseph Redman; Robert A. Roberts; John Sellers; Nathan Sellers; Samuel Sellers; John Shaw Jr.; Walter Shee; Jonathan Bayard Smith (member of the Continental Congress); Thomas Smith; Robert Tuckniss; Andrew Tybout; Joseph Watkins Jr.; William Webb; Israel Whelen. *See appendix A for more information.*

W-8531 • **$1** • 138,889 printed. Nature printing: One ragweed leaf and two willow leaves.

Signed by
Andrew Tybout and Josiah Hewes.

	VG-8	F-12	VF-20	EF-40	AU-50	Unc-63	Unc-65
2009	$90	$150	$250	$350	$450	$1,000	$1,650
2020	$125	$150	$250	$500	$750	$2,500	$4,000

Values for notes above $100 are for certified (professionally graded) pieces.

W-8532 • $2 • 138,889 printed. Nature printing: One raspberry leaf and two filbert leaves.

**Signed by
George Campbell and Daniel Clymer.**

	VG-8	F-12	VF-20	EF-40	AU-50	Unc-63	Unc-65
2009	$90	$150	$250	$350	$450	$1,000	$1,650
2020	$100	$125	$150	$400	$600	$2,000	$3,500

Values for notes above $100 are for certified (professionally graded) pieces.

W-8533 • $3 • 138,889 printed. Nature printing: Elm leaf section and wings from a maple seed.

**Signed by
Nicholas Garrison and John Howard.**

	VG-8	F-12	VF-20	EF-40	AU-50	Unc-63	Unc-65
2009	$90	$150	$250	$350	$450	$1,000	$1,650
2020	$100	$125	$150	$350	$500	$1,500	$3,000

Values for notes above $100 are for certified (professionally graded) pieces.

W-8534 • $4 • 138,889 printed. Nature printing: Sections of wings from a maple seed. On this bill the bottom vignette is oriented upward instead of facing toward the center as on all other bills.

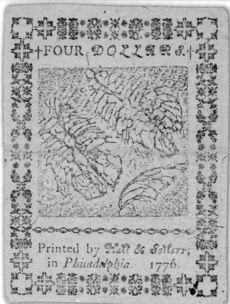

Signed by
Joseph Parker and Robert Evans.

	VG-8	F-12	VF-20	EF-40	AU-50	Unc-63	Unc-65
2009	$90	$150	$250	$350	$450	$1,000	$1,650
2020	$100	$125	$150	$350	$500	$1,500	$3,000

Values for notes above $100 are for certified (professionally graded) pieces.

W-8535 • $5 • 138,889 printed. Nature printing: Betony and sage leaves.

Signed by
James Johnston and Philip Kinsey.

	VG-8	F-12	VF-20	EF-40	AU-50	Unc-63	Unc-65
2009	$90	$150	$250	$350	$450	$1,000	$1,650
2020	$100	$125	$150	$350	$500	$1,500	$3,000

Values for notes above $100 are for certified (professionally graded) pieces.

W-8536 • $6 • 138,889 printed. Nature printing: Prominent buttercup leaf.

**Signed by
Benjamin Brannan and Samuel Sellers.**

	VG-8	F-12	VF-20	EF-40	AU-50	Unc-63	Unc-65
2009	$90	$150	$250	$350	$450	$1,000	$1,650
2020	$100	$125	$150	$350	$500	$1,500	$3,000

Values for notes above $100 are for certified (professionally graded) pieces.

W-8537 • **$7** • 138,889 printed. Nature printing: Prominent buttercup leaf, differently oriented.

Signed by
James Johnston and John Howard.

	VG-8	F-12	VF-20	EF-40	AU-50	Unc-63	Unc-65
2009	$90	$150	$250	$350	$450	$1,000	$1,650
2020	$100	$125	$150	$350	$500	$1,500	$3,000

Values for notes above $100 are for certified (professionally graded) pieces.

W-8538 • $8 • 138,889 printed. Nature printing: Prominent buttercup leaf and two smaller leaves.

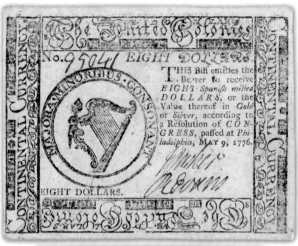

Signed by
Joseph Parker and Robert Evans.

	VG-8	F-12	VF-20	EF-40	AU-50	Unc-63	Unc-65
2009	$90	$150	$250	$350	$450	$1,000	$1,650
2020	$100	$125	$150	$350	$500	$1,500	$3,000

Values for notes above $100 are for certified (professionally graded) pieces.

July 22, 1776

Authorized amount: $5,000,000
Imprinted Philadelphia

Authorized on two dates, July 22 and August 13, 1776, but the bills are all imprinted July 22, 1776. The $1 denomination was not used, possibly as metallic dollars were being made. Sheets were printed on blue paper to aid in the detection of counterfeits.

KNOWN SIGNERS OF THE JULY 22, 1776, BILLS

James Ash; John Boyd; Benjamin Brannan; Joseph Bullock; Daniel Clymer; Thomas Donellan; Nicholas Garrison; George Gray Jr.; Josiah Hewes; Samuel Hillegas; John Howard; Isaac Howell; Benjamin Jacobs; Rinaldo Johnson; Philip Kinsey; Thomas Leech; Jacob (Samuel) Massey; William Masters; Anthony Morris Jr.; Samuel C. Morris; John Ord; Joseph Parker; Isaac Pearson; Joseph Redman; T. Russell (Rusell); John Saltar (Salter); John Sellers; Nathan Sellers; Samuel Sellers; John Shee; Walter Shee; Jonathan Bayard Smith (member of the Continental Congress); R. Smith; D. Stewart (Stuart); Andrew Tybout; James Walker; Joseph Watkins Jr.; William Webb; Israel Whelen; John Williams. *See appendix A for more information.*

W-8539 • **$2** • 76,923 printed. Nature printing: One raspberry leaf and two filbert leaves.

**Signed by
Anthony Morris Jr. and Benjamin Brannan.**

	VG-8	F-12	VF-20	EF-40	AU-50	Unc-63	Unc-65
2009	$100	$195	$275	$350	$450	$1,200	$2,000
2020	$200	$300	$350	$750	$1,500	$3,000	$4,500

Values for notes above $100 are for certified (professionally graded) pieces.

W-8540 • **$3** • 76,923 printed. Nature printing: Elm leaf section and wings from a maple seed.

Signed by
Nathan Sellers and Joseph Watkins.

	VG-8	F-12	VF-20	EF-40	AU-50	Unc-63	Unc-65
2009	$100	$195	$275	$350	$450	$1,200	$2,000
2020	$150	$250	$300	$600	$1,000	$2,000	$4,000

Values for notes above $100 are for certified (professionally graded) pieces.

W-8541 • **$4** • 76,923 printed. Nature printing: Sections of wings from a maple seed.

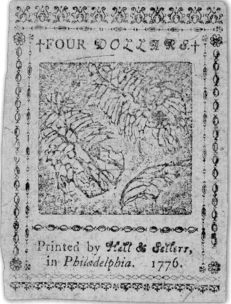

**Signed by
John Howard and Benjamin Brannan.**

	VG-8	F-12	VF-20	EF-40	AU-50	Unc-63	Unc-65
2009	$100	$195	$275	$350	$450	$1,200	$2,000
2020	$150	$250	$300	$600	$1,000	$2,000	$4,000

Values for notes above $100 are for certified (professionally graded) pieces.

W-8542 • **$5** • 76,923 printed. Nature printing: Betony and sage leaves. In the motto the word ABSTINE has the B erroneously cut backwards, then corrected, giving it the appearance of an H. This identical engraving element was used on $5 bills of the next two issues.

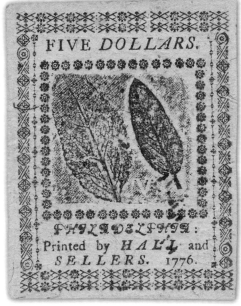

Signed by
Walter Shee and William Webb.

	VG-8	F-12	VF-20	EF-40	AU-50	Unc-63	Unc-65
2009	$100	$195	$275	$350	$450	$1,200	$2,000
2020	$150	$250	$300	$600	$1,000	$2,000	$4,000

Values for notes above $100 are for certified (professionally graded) pieces.

W-8543 • $6 • 76,923 printed. Nature printing: Prominent buttercup leaf.

Signed by
Israel Whelen and Benjamin Jacobs.

	VG-8	F-12	VF-20	EF-40	AU-50	Unc-63	Unc-65
2009	$100	$195	$275	$350	$450	$1,200	$2,000
2020	$150	$250	$300	$600	$1,000	$2,000	$4,000

Values for notes above $100 are for certified (professionally graded) pieces.

W-8544 • **$7** • 76,923 printed. Nature printing: Prominent buttercup leaf, differently oriented.

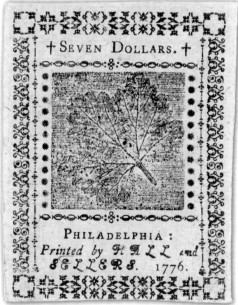

Signed by
Nicholas Garrison and John Howard.

	VG-8	F-12	VF-20	EF-40	AU-50	Unc-63	Unc-65
2009	$100	$195	$275	$350	$450	$1,200	$2,000
2020	$150	$250	$300	$600	$1,000	$2,000	$4,000

Values for notes above $100 are for certified (professionally graded) pieces.

W-8545 • **$8** • 76,923 printed. Nature printing: Prominent buttercup leaf and two smaller leaves.

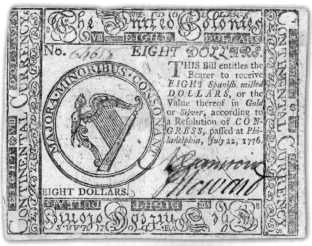

Signed by
Nicholas Garrison and John Howard.

	VG-8	F-12	VF-20	EF-40	AU-50	Unc-63	Unc-65
2009	$100	$195	$275	$350	$450	$1,200	$2,000
2020	$150	$250	$300	$600	$1,000	$2,000	$4,000

Values for notes above $100 are for certified (professionally graded) pieces.

W-8546 • **$30** • 76,923 printed. Wind blowing on rough sea; sun over sea with two sailing ships.

**Signed by
William Masters and John Williams.**

	VG-8	F-12	VF-20	EF-40	AU-50	Unc-63	Unc-65
2009	$125	$225	$300	$450	$600	$1,500	$2,750
2020	$150	$250	$300	$600	$1,000	$2,000	$4,000

Values for notes above $100 are for certified (professionally graded) pieces.

November 2, 1776

**Authorized amount: $5,000,000 plus $500,000
for fractional bills (never issued)
Imprinted Philadelphia**

Authorized on two dates, November 2 and December 28, 1776, but the bills are all imprinted November 2, 1776. Sheets of blue paper were printed for counterfeit detection.

KNOWN SIGNERS OF THE NOVEMBER 2, 1776, BILLS

William Adcock; William Asquith; Mark Alexander; John (Joshua) Barney; Theodore Barrel; John Boyd; Benjamin Brannan; Clement Brooks (Brook, Brooke); James Calhoun (Colhoun); Daniel Carroll; John Cockey (Cokey); Hercules Courtenay (Courtney); Hans Creery (Creevy); Richard Cromwell; Thomas Donellan; Caleb Dorsey; John Dorsey; Robert Dorsey; James Franklin; Joseph Gaither; William Gibson; William Govett; Dennis Griffith; John Griffiths (Griffith); William Hammond; Samuel Hillegas; Richard Johns; John (James) Kelso; Benjamin Levy; Darby Lux; Zachariah Maccubin (Mackubin); Aquila Norris; George Patterson; St. George Peale; T. Peters; Frederick Phyle (Phile); John Philpot; Richard Stringer; John Taylor; James Walker; George Welch; William Young. *See appendix A for more information.*

W-8547 • **$2** • 76,923 printed. Nature printing: One raspberry leaf and two filbert leaves.

**Signed by
Benjamin Levy and Thomas Donellan.**

	VG-8	F-12	VF-20	EF-40	AU-50	Unc-63	Unc-65
2009	$90	$165	$265	$350	$450	$1,200	$2,000
2020	$150	$200	$300	$750	$1,500	$2,500	$4,000

Values for notes above $100 are for certified (professionally graded) pieces.

W-8548 • **$3** • 76,923 printed. Nature printing: Elm leaf section and wings from a maple seed.

**Signed by
Joseph Gaither and Thomas Donellan.**

	VG-8	F-12	VF-20	EF-40	AU-50	Unc-63	Unc-65
2009	$90	$165	$265	$350	$450	$1,200	$2,000
2020	$100	$125	$175	$400	$750	$2,000	$3,500

Values for notes above $100 are for certified (professionally graded) pieces.

W-8549 • **$4** • 76,923 printed. Nature printing: Sections of wings from a maple seed.

Signed by
Joseph Gaither and Dennis Griffith.

	VG-8	F-12	VF-20	EF-40	AU-50	Unc-63	Unc-65
2009	$90	$165	$265	$350	$450	$1,200	$2,000
2020	$100	$125	$175	$400	$750	$2,000	$3,500

Values for notes above $100 are for certified (professionally graded) pieces.

W-8550 • $5 • 76,923 printed. Nature printing: Betony and sage leaves.

Signed by
Joseph Gaither and Dennis Griffith.

	VG-8	F-12	VF-20	EF-40	AU-50	Unc-63	Unc-65
2009	$90	$165	$265	$350	$450	$1,200	$2,000
2020	$100	$125	$175	$400	$750	$2,000	$3,500

Values for notes above $100 are for certified (professionally graded) pieces.

W-8551 • **$6** • 76,923 printed. Nature printing: Prominent buttercup leaf.

Signed by
John Griffith and William Asquith.

	VG-8	F-12	VF-20	EF-40	AU-50	Unc-63	Unc-65
2009	$90	$165	$265	$350	$450	$1,200	$2,000
2020	$100	$125	$175	$400	$750	$2,000	$3,500

Values for notes above $100 are for certified (professionally graded) pieces.

W-8552 • $7 • 76,923 printed. Nature printing: Prominent buttercup leaf, differently oriented.

**Signed by
Joseph Gaither and Richard Cromwell.**

	VG-8	F-12	VF-20	EF-40	AU-50	Unc-63	Unc-65
2009	$90	$165	$265	$350	$450	$1,200	$2,000
2020	$100	$125	$175	$400	$750	$2,000	$3,500

Values for notes above $100 are for certified (professionally graded) pieces.

W-8553 • **$8** • 76,923 printed. Nature printing: Prominent buttercup leaf and two smaller leaves.

Signed by
Benjamin Brannan and Samuel Hillegas.

	VG-8	F-12	VF-20	EF-40	AU-50	Unc-63	Unc-65
2009	$90	$165	$265	$350	$450	$1,200	$2,000
2020	$100	$125	$175	$400	$750	$2,000	$3,500

Values for notes above $100 are for certified (professionally graded) pieces.

W-8554 • **$30** • 76,923 printed. Wind blowing on rough sea; sun over sea with two sailing ships.

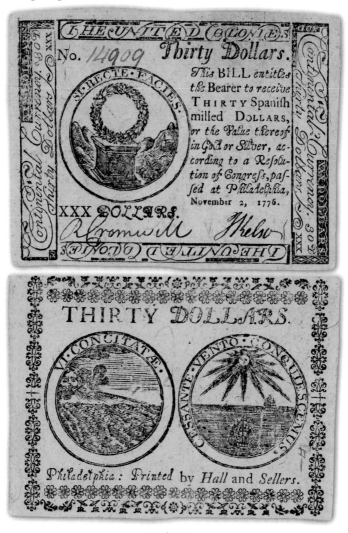

Signed by
Richard Cromwell and John Kelso.

	VG-8	F-12	VF-20	EF-40	AU-50	Unc-63	Unc-65
2009	$90	$165	$265	$350	$450	$1,200	$2,000
2020	$125	$150	$200	$500	$1,000	$2,500	$4,000

Values for notes above $100 are for certified (professionally graded) pieces.

February 26, 1777

Authorized amount: $5,000,000
Imprinted Baltimore

This resolution was passed in Baltimore, where the Continental Congress met by necessity, for the British occupied Philadelphia from December 20, 1776, until February 27, 1777. The imprint of Hall & Sellers on the back eliminated the standard PHILADELPHIA, and no address was given. Eric Newman states that the printers were able to return to Philadelphia on March 4, 1777, and that most or all of the bills of this authorization were printed there.

KNOWN SIGNERS OF THE FEBRUARY 26, 1777, BILLS

William Adcock; William Asquith; Charles Alexander; John (Joshua) Barney; R. Buchanan; Daniel Carroll; Samuel Stringer Coale; W. Coale; Hans Creery (Creevy); Richard Cromwell; Thomas Donellan; Robert Dorsey; Dennis Griffith; John Griffiths (Griffith); Horatio Johnson; Rinaldo Johnson; John (James) Kelso; Benjamin Levy; C. Lewis; Zachariah Maccubin (Mackubin); John McHenry; Aquila Norris; St. George Peale; R. Smith; William Spear; John Taylor; James Walker; George Welch. *See appendix A for more information.*

W-8555 • $2 • 76,923 printed. Nature printing: One raspberry leaf and two filbert leaves.

Signed by
John (Joshua) Barney and Thomas Donellan.

	VG-8	F-12	VF-20	EF-40	AU-50	Unc-63	Unc-65
2009	$100	$175	$250	$375	$475	$1,200	$1,900
2020	$150	$200	$300	$750	$1,250	$2,500	$4,500

Values for notes above $100 are for certified (professionally graded) pieces.

W-8556 • $3 • 76,923 printed. Nature printing: Elm leaf section and wings from a maple seed.

Signed by
George Welch and Thomas Donellan.

	VG-8	F-12	VF-20	EF-40	AU-50	Unc-63	Unc-65
2009	$100	$175	$250	$375	$475	$1,200	$1,900
2020	$100	$125	$175	$350	$600	$2,000	$3,750

Values for notes above $100 are for certified (professionally graded) pieces.

W-8557 • $4 • 76,923 printed. Nature printing: Sections of wings from a maple seed.

**Signed by
John Taylor and Aquila Norris.**

	VG-8	F-12	VF-20	EF-40	AU-50	Unc-63	Unc-65
2009	$100	$175	$250	$375	$475	$1,200	$1,900
2020	$100	$125	$175	$350	$600	$2,000	$3,750

Values for notes above $100 are for certified (professionally graded) pieces.

W-8558 • **$5** • 76,923 printed. Nature printing: Betony and sage leaves.

Signed by
John Kelso and Richard Cromwell.

	VG-8	F-12	VF-20	EF-40	AU-50	Unc-63	Unc-65
2009	$100	$175	$250	$375	$475	$1,200	$1,900
2020	$100	$125	$175	$350	$600	$2,000	$3,750

Values for notes above $100 are for certified (professionally graded) pieces.

W-8559 • **$6** • 76,923 printed. Nature printing: Prominent buttercup leaf.

Signed by
James Walker and Horatio Johnson.

	VG-8	F-12	VF-20	EF-40	AU-50	Unc-63	Unc-65
2009	$100	$175	$250	$375	$475	$1,200	$1,900
2020	$100	$125	$175	$350	$600	$2,000	$3,750

Values for notes above $100 are for certified (professionally graded) pieces.

W-8560 • **$7** • 76,923 printed. Nature printing: Prominent buttercup leaf differently oriented.

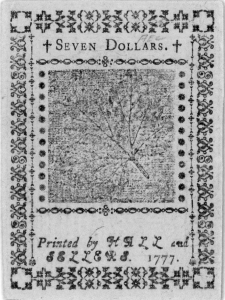

Signed by
James Walker and Horatio Johnson.

	VG-8	F-12	VF-20	EF-40	AU-50	Unc-63	Unc-65
2009	$100	$175	$250	$375	$475	$1,200	$1,900
2020	$100	$125	$175	$350	$600	$2,000	$3,750

Values for notes above $100 are for certified (professionally graded) pieces.

W-8561 • $8 • 76,923 printed. Nature printing: Prominent buttercup leaf and two smaller leaves.

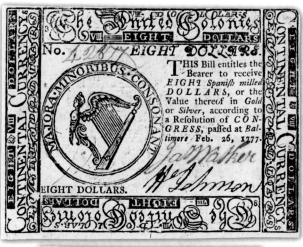

Signed by
James Walker and Horatio Johnson.

	VG-8	F-12	VF-20	EF-40	AU-50	Unc-63	Unc-65
2009	$100	$175	$250	$375	$475	$1,200	$1,900
2020	$100	$125	$175	$350	$600	$2,000	$3,750

Values for notes above $100 are for certified (professionally graded) pieces.

W-8562 • $30 • 76,923 printed. Wind blowing on rough sea; sun over sea with two sailing ships.

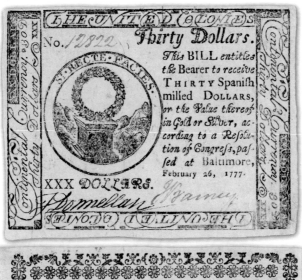

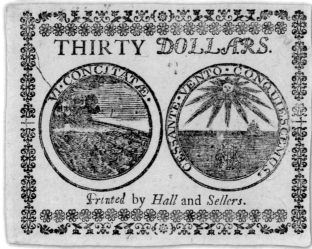

Signed by
Thomas Donellan and John (Joshua) Barney.

	VG-8	F-12	VF-20	EF-40	AU-50	Unc-63	Unc-65
2009	$125	$200	$300	$450	$525	$1,500	$2,250
2020	$125	$200	$300	$750	$1,250	$3,000	$4,000

Values for notes above $100 are for certified (professionally graded) pieces.

May 20, 1777

Authorized amount: $16,500,000

Imprinted Philadelphia

Although the bills are all dated May 20, 1777, the large amount was authorized in 10 separate resolutions extended to April 18, 1778. From this issue onward the bills were imprinted United States instead of United Colonies. This issue was extensively counterfeited. This and the next issue were called in by the Treasury to be exchanged for other bills by the first day of June 1778. Many bills were exchanged by then, after which they would not be redeemed.[5] Bills of these two issues were thus discredited, and many people refused to accept them. Some bills were printed on sheets of blue paper for counterfeit detection purposes.

KNOWN SIGNERS OF THE MAY 20, 1777, BILLS

William Adcock; J. Billmeyer Aisquith; S. Bryson; G. Budd; Levi Budd; James Calhoun (Colhoun); R.(H.) Christ Jr.; J. Chrysiler; Charles Cist; James Claypoole; Samuel Stringer Coale; W. Coale; Hans Creery (Creevy); Richard Cromwell; Thomas Donellan; George Eichelberger; S. Elms.; James Ewing; William Govett; M. Hahn; William Hardy; Casper Hiener; Joseph Hiester; Samuel Hillegas; T. Hopkinson; J. Houston; Robert Irwin; Horatio Johnson; Rinaldo Johnson; J. Kean; Frederick Kuhl; J. Kuhn; Peter Kurtz; G.L. Lester; Daniel Levan; Benjamin Levy; C. Lewis; M. Mahon; R. McAlester; A. McCallister (Macallister); Aquila Norris; Joseph Nourse; I. Paisley; C. Parr; St. George Peale; Joseph Pennell (Pennel); T. Peters; James Ross; J. Rothrock; William Scott; Charles Shoemaker; J. Short; Belcher Peartree Smith; R. Smith; Jedediah Snowden; William Spear; T. Sweeney (Sweney); John Taylor; F. Wade; Thomas Warren; J. Watson; George Welch; John Wright; Moses Young. *See appendix A for more information.*

W-8563 • **$2** • 253,850 printed. Nature printing: One raspberry leaf and two filbert leaves.

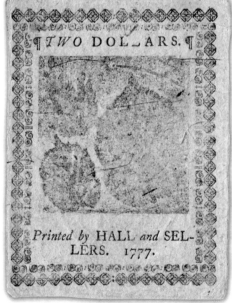

Signed by
C. Parr and J. Kuhn.

	VG-8	F-12	VF-20	EF-40	AU-50	Unc-63	Unc-65
2009	$150	$300	$600	$900	$1,250	$2,800	$3,500
2020	$400	$600	$750	$2,500	$3,500		

Values for notes above $100 are for certified (professionally graded) pieces.

W-8564 • $3 • 253,839 printed. Nature printing: Elm leaf section and wings from a maple seed.

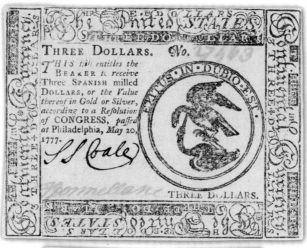

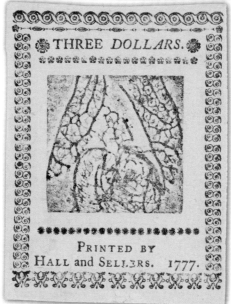

Signed by
Samuel Stringer Coale and Thomas Donellan.

	VG-8	F-12	VF-20	EF-40	AU-50	Unc-63	Unc-65
2009	$150	$300	$600	$900	$1,250	$2,800	$3,500
2020	$250	$500	$600	$1,750	$2,500		

Values for notes above $100 are for certified (professionally graded) pieces.

W-8565 • **$4** • 253,839 printed. Nature printing: Sections of wings from a maple seed.

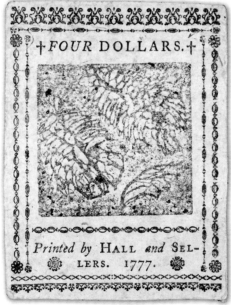

Signed by
Casper Hiener and Thomas Warren.

	VG-8	F-12	VF-20	EF-40	AU-50	Unc-63	Unc-65
2009	$150	$300	$600	$900	$1,250	$2,800	$3,500
2020	$250	$350	$450	$750	$1,000	$3,500	$5,000

Values for notes above $100 are for certified (professionally graded) pieces.

W-8566 • **$5** • 253,840 printed. Nature printing: Betony and sage leaves.

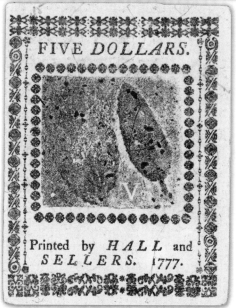

**Signed by
M. Hahn and J. Houston.**

	VG-8	F-12	VF-20	EF-40	AU-50	Unc-63	Unc-65
2009	$150	$300	$600	$900	$1,250	$2,800	$3,500
2020	$250	$350	$450	$750	$1,000	$3,500	$5,000

Values for notes above $100 are for certified (professionally graded) pieces.

W-8567 • **$6** • 253,839 printed. Nature printing: Prominent buttercup leaf.

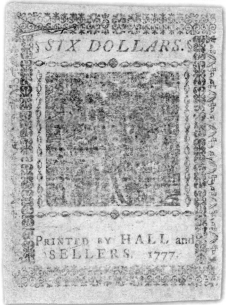

Signed by
James Ross and Peter Kurtz.

	VG-8	F-12	VF-20	EF-40	AU-50	Unc-63	Unc-65
2009	$150	$300	$600	$900	$1,250	$2,800	$3,500
2020	$250	$350	$450	$750	$1,000	$3,500	$5,000

Values for notes above $100 are for certified (professionally graded) pieces.

W-8568 • **$7** • 253,840 printed. Nature printing: Prominent buttercup leaf, differently oriented.

Signed by
[illegible].

	VG-8	F-12	VF-20	EF-40	AU-50	Unc-63	Unc-65
2009	$150	$300	$600	$900	$1,250	$2,800	$3,500
2020	$250	$350	$450	$750	$1,000	$3,500	$5,000

Values for notes above $100 are for certified (professionally graded) pieces.

W-8569 • **$8** • 253,851 printed. Nature printing: Prominent buttercup leaf and two smaller leaves.

**Signed by
Charles Cist and J. Billmeyer.**

	VG-8	F-12	VF-20	EF-40	AU-50	Unc-63	Unc-65
2009	$150	$300	$600	$900	$1,250	$2,800	$3,500
2020	$250	$350	$450	$750	$1,000	$3,500	$5,000

Values for notes above $100 are for certified (professionally graded) pieces.

W-8570 • $30 • 253,850 printed. Wind blowing on rough sea; sun over sea with two sailing ships.

Signed by
Charles Cist and J. Rothrock.

	VG-8	F-12	VF-20	EF-40	AU-50	Unc-63	Unc-65
2009	$200	$350	$700	$1,000	$1,500	$3,450	$4,500
2020	$250	$350	$450	$750	$1,000	$3,500	$5,000

Values for notes above $100 are for certified (professionally graded) pieces.

April 11, 1778

Authorized amount: $25,000,000
Imprinted York Town

Authorized by multiple acts at York ("York-town" on the bills), Pennsylvania, on April 11 and other times, and in Philadelphia, but all imprinted April 11, 1778. Congress met in York from September 30, 1777, to June 27, 1778, Hall & Sellers set up printing facilities there on the southwest corner of Market and Beaver streets.[6] The backs of the bills eliminate Philadelphia and give no address for the firm. As a class, currency of this series is rarer than any other issue, as many bills were called back to be replaced with other bills, in view of widespread counterfeiting. The $40 denomination was introduced with a new emblem. The depreciation of Continental Currency made it economical to create higher denominations, as was done increasingly from this point to the end of the series.

KNOWN SIGNERS OF THE APRIL 11, 1778, BILLS

William Adcock; Samuel Baird; J. Billmeyer; S. Bryson; Robert Caither (Cather); Charles Cist; N. Cranch; Nathaniel Donnell; Henry Eyres; Lewis Farmer; Edwin (Edward) Fox; J. Garrigues; William Hardy; C. Herandez; John Howard; Joseph Hubley; Peter Kurtz; James Little; C. Mitchel; W. Momegan; Frederick Phyle (Phile); D. Reintzel; Robert A. Roberts; James Ross; J. Rothrock; James Rowan; William Rush; E. Ryves; Jedediah Snowden; Joseph Snowden; William Thorn (Thorne); James Wilson (member of the Continental Congress; signer of the Declaration of Independence[7]); Joseph Wilson; John Wright; John Young Jr. *See appendix A for more information.*

W-8571 • **$4** • 208,335 printed. Nature printing: Prominent buttercup leaf.

**Signed by
Peter Kurtz and J. Rothrock.**

	VG-8	F-12	VF-20	EF-40	AU-50	Unc-63
2009	$275	$450	$750	$1,200	$2,000	$4,000
2020	$500	$1,000	$1,500	$3,000	$4,500	

Values for notes above $100 are for certified (professionally graded) pieces.

W-8572 • **$5** • 208,330 printed. Nature printing: Two crossed willow leaves.

Signed by
James Ross and [faded].

	VG-8	F-12	VF-20	EF-40	AU-50	Unc-63	Unc-65
2009	$275	$450	$750	$1,200	$2,000	$4,000	
2020	$300	$750	$750	$2,000	$3,500	$5,000	$7,500

Values for notes above $100 are for certified (professionally graded) pieces.

W-8573 • $6 • 208,335 printed. Nature printing: Sage leaf. The illustrated bill is an excellent example of hasty cutting with scissors.

**Signed by
D. Reintzel and S. Bryson.**

	VG-8	F-12	VF-20	EF-40	AU-50	Unc-63	Unc-65
2009	$275	$450	$750	$1,200	$2,000	$4,000	
2020	$300	$500	$500	$750	$1,250	$4,000	$6,000

Values for notes above $100 are for certified (professionally graded) pieces.

W-8574 • **$7** • 208,330 printed. Nature printing: Two leaves, sage and grape.

Signed by
Joseph Hubley and Robert A. Roberts.

	VG-8	F-12	VF-20	EF-40	AU-50	Unc-63	Unc-65
2009	$275	$450	$750	$1,200	$2,000	$4,000	
2020	$300	$400	$500	$750	$1,250	$4,000	$6,000

Values for notes above $100 are for certified (professionally graded) pieces.

W-8575 • **$8** • 208,330 printed. Nature printing: Prominent buttercup leaf and two smaller leaves.

Signed by
James Rowan and James Little.

	VG-8	F-12	VF-20	EF-40	AU-50	Unc-63	Unc-65
2009	$275	$450	$750	$1,200	$2,000	$4,000	
2020	$300	$400	$500	$750	$1,250	$4,000	$6,000

Values for notes above $100 are for certified (professionally graded) pieces.

W-8576 • $20 • 208,330 printed. Nature printing: Prominent buttercup leaf.

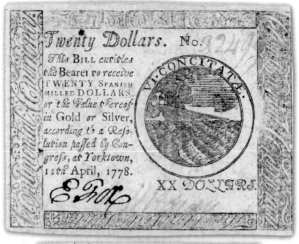

Signed by
Edwin Fox and William Hardy.

	VG-8	F-12	VF-20	EF-40	AU-50	Unc-63	Unc-65
2009	$275	$450	$750	$1,200	$2,000	$4,000	
2020	$300	$400	$500	$750	$1,250	$4,000	$6,000

Values for notes above $100 are for certified (professionally graded) pieces.

W-8577 • **$30** • 208,335 printed. Nature printing: Three willow leaves.

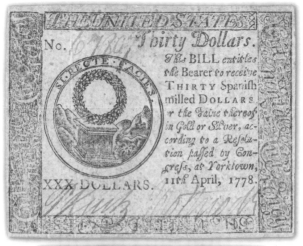

Signed by
Peter Kurtz and J. Rothrock.

	VG-8	F-12	VF-20	EF-40	AU-50	Unc-63	Unc-65
2009	$275	$450	$750	$1,200	$2,000	$4,000	
2020	$300	$400	$500	$750	$1,250	$4,000	$6,000

Values for notes above $100 are for certified (professionally graded) pieces.

W-8578 • **$40** • 208,335 printed. Nature printing: Carrot leaf and two smaller leaves. The face design was created by Francis Hopkinson for use on this new denomination.

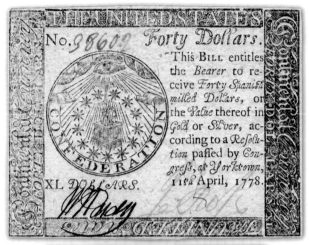

Signed by
William Hardy and J. Rothrock.

	VG-8	F-12	VF-20	EF-40	AU-50	Unc-63	Unc-65
2009	$275	$450	$750	$1,200	$2,000	$4,000	
2020	$400	$500	$750	$1,500	$2,000	$4,500	$6,500

Values for notes above $100 are for certified (professionally graded) pieces.

September 26, 1778

Authorized amount: $75,001,080

Imprinted Philadelphia

These bills were issued under nine different resolutions, but all are dated September 26, 1778. This authorization was for a greater amount of money than all previous issues combined. The $50 and $60 denominations were introduced in this series and have emblems created by Francis Hopkinson. Sheets of bills were printed on blue paper for counterfeit detection purposes.

Known Signers of the September 26, 1778, Bills

William Adcock; Charles Alexander; Isaac All; Christopher Charles; Gunning (Emmery) Bedford Jr. (member of the Continental Congress; signer of the Constitution); George Bond; George Bright; S. Bryson (such bills are counterfeit, per an interpretation of Newman); Levi Budd; Joseph Carleton; Robert Cather (Caither); William Coats; Joseph Coit; William Colladay; Cornelius Comegys; Paul Cox; N. Cranch; Nathaniel Donnell, James Dundas; Thomas Edison (Eddison); S. Elms; Henry Epplé; Richard Eyres; Lewis Farmer; Patrick Ferrall; William Gamble (Gauble); Joseph Gardner (member of the Continental Congress); J. Garrigues; Jacob Graff; John Graff Jr.; Isaac Gray; William Gray; M. Hahn; William Hardy; John Helm; C. Herandez; Henry Kammerer; John (Joseph) Kerr (Ker); Michael Kimmell; John Laurence (Lawrence); John Leacock; James Little; Samuel Lyon; William Marshall; Jacob Masoner; Robert Mullen (Mullan); Thomas Nevill (Nevell); Samuel Nicholas; John Nicholson; Joseph Nourse; John Read (Reed); Robert Roberts Jr.; James Ross; Hampton Round (Rownd); James Rowan; William Rush; E. Ryves; Michael Shubart; Luson (Ludson) Simmons; R. Smith; John Smyth; Jedediah Snowden; Joseph Snowden; Ludovic Sprogell; William Stretch; Francis Swaine; John Thomson; Joseph Walter; Joseph Watkins Jr.; Samuel Wetherell (Wetherill) Jr.; John Williams (member of the Continental Congress); Joseph Wilson; Daniel Wistar (Wister); John Wright. *See appendix A for more information.*

W-8579 • **$5** • 340,914 printed. Nature printing: Two crossed willow leaves.

Signed by
Richard Eyres and William Hardy.

	VG-8	F-12	VF-20	EF-40	AU-50	Unc-63	Unc-65
2009	$80	$125	$175	$275	$350	$800	$1,300
2020	$100	$125	$150	$300	$500	$1,500	$3,000

Values for notes above $100 are for certified (professionally graded) pieces.

W-8580 • **$7** • 340,914 printed. Nature printing: Prominent buttercup leaf.

Signed by
William Gamble and J. Snowden.

	VG-8	F-12	VF-20	EF-40	AU-50	Unc-63	Unc-65
2009	$80	$125	$175	$275	$350	$800	$1,300
2020	$100	$125	$150	$225	$400	$1,000	$2,000

Values for notes above $100 are for certified (professionally graded) pieces.

W-8581 • **$8** • 340,914 printed. Nature printing: Prominent buttercup leaf and two smaller leaves.

Signed by
Paul Cox and Nathaniel Donnell.

	VG-8	F-12	VF-20	EF-40	AU-50	Unc-63	Unc-65
2009	$80	$125	$175	$275	$350	$800	$1,300
2020	$100	$125	$150	$225	$400	$1,000	$2,000

Values for notes above $100 are for certified (professionally graded) pieces.

W-8582 • $20 • 340,914 printed. Nature printing: Prominent butter cup leaf.

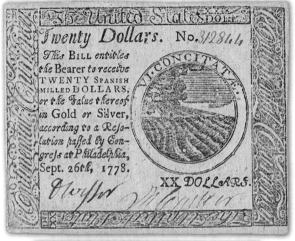

Signed by
D. Wistar and R. Cather.

	VG-8	F-12	VF-20	EF-40	AU-50	Unc-63	Unc-65
2009	$80	$125	$175	$275	$350	$800	$1,300
2020	$100	$125	$150	$225	$400	$1,000	$2,000

Values for notes above $100 are for certified (professionally graded) pieces.

W-8583 • **$30** • 340,914 printed. Nature printing: Three willow leaves.

Signed by
Samuel Lyon and Robert Roberts.

	VG-8	F-12	VF-20	EF-40	AU-50	Unc-63	Unc-65
2009	$80	$125	$175	$275	$350	$800	$1,300
2020	$100	$125	$150	$225	$400	$1,000	$2,000

Values for notes above $100 are for certified (professionally graded) pieces.

W-8584 • **$40** • 340,914 printed. Carrot leaf and two smaller leaves.

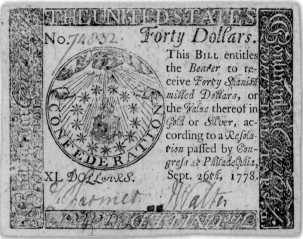

Signed by
Lewis Farmer and Joseph Walter.

	VG-8	F-12	VF-20	EF-40	AU-50	Unc-63	Unc-65
2009	$80	$125	$175	$275	$350	$800	$1,300
2020	$100	$125	$150	$225	$400	$1,000	$2,000

Values for notes above $100 are for certified (professionally graded) pieces.

W-8585 • **$50** • 340,914 printed. Three arrows.

Signed by
D. Wistar and R. Cather.

	VG-8	F-12	VF-20	EF-40	AU-50	Unc-63	Unc-65
2009	$80	$125	$175	$275	$350	$800	$1,300
2020	$125	$150	$175	$250	$450	$1,000	$2,000

Values for notes above $100 are for certified (professionally graded) pieces.

W-8586 • $60 • 340,914 printed. Stringed bow.

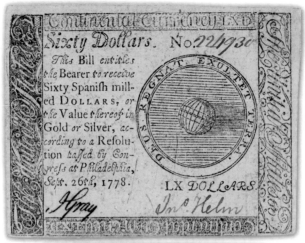

Signed by
Isaac Gray and John Helm.

	VG-8	F-12	VF-20	EF-40	AU-50	Unc-63	Unc-65
2009	$80	$125	$175	$275	$350	$800	$1,300
2020	$125	$150	$175	$250	$450	$1,250	$2,500

Values for notes above $100 are for certified (professionally graded) pieces.

January 14, 1779

Authorized amount: $95,051,695

Imprinted Philadelphia

Authorized by nine different resolutions, but all dated January 14, 1779. By this time Continental Currency had depreciated to be worth pennies on the dollar. This is the final series and also the most extensive in terms of different denominations, including the new values of $65, $70, and $80. On the face of each bill certain elements were printed in red to deter counterfeiting. $30 to $65 bills were printed on sheets watermarked CONFEDERATION in two lines. Sheets for anti-counterfeiting purposes were printed in black and red ink on blue paper.

These were to remain legal tender until January 1, 1797. The public viewed these deeply depreciated bills as being nearly worthless, despite many newspaper articles proclaiming them to be safe and solid.[8] Generally, bills of this series are found in relatively higher grades as they did not circulate for a long time.

KNOWN SIGNERS OF THE JANUARY 14, 1779, BILLS

Christopher (Charles) Baker; Thomas Barclay; George Bond; George Bright; Levi Budd; Joseph Carleton; Robert Cather (Caither); William Coats; Joseph Coit; William Colladay; Cornelius Comegys; Paul Cox; Nathaniel Donnell; James Dundas; Thomas Edison (Eddison); Henry Epplé; Patrick Ferrall; Joseph Gaither; William Gamble (Gauble); Joseph Gardner (member of the Continental Congress); Jacob Graff; John Graff Jr.; Isaac Gray; William Gray; John Helm; John (Joseph) Kerr (Ker); Michael Kimmell; Laurence (Lawrence); John Leacock; Samuel Lyon; Jacob Masoner; Robert Mullen (Mullan); Samuel Nicholas; Joseph Nourse; John William Ramsey (Ramsay); John Read (Reed); Robert A. Roberts; Jacob Schreiner; Luson (Ludson) Simmons; Jedediah Snowden; Joseph Snowden; Ludovic Sprogell; William Stretch; Francis Swaine; Joseph Watkins Jr.; Samuel Wetherell (Wetherill) Jr.; John Williams (member of the Continental Congress); James Wilson (member of the Continental Congress; signer of the Declaration of Independence)[9]; Daniel Wistar (Wister). *See appendix A for more information.*

W-8587 • **$1** • 139,811 printed. Nature printing: Tansy leaf.

Signed by
Jacob Graff and Michael Kimmell.

	VG-8	F-12	VF-20	EF-40	AU-50	Unc-63	Unc-65
2009	$80	$100	$175	$240	$350	$950	$1,600
2020	$125	$150	$250	$600	$1,250	$2,500	$4,000

Values for notes above $100 are for certified (professionally graded) pieces.

W-8588 • $2 • 139,811 printed. Nature printing: Mulberry leaf.

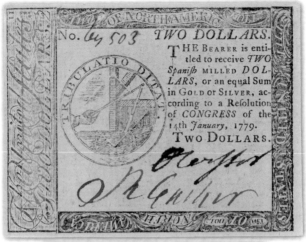

Signed by
D. Wistar and Joseph Gaither.

	VG-8	F-12	VF-20	EF-40	AU-50	Unc-63	Unc-65
2009	$70	$85	$150	$200	$275	$625	$1,250
2020	$100	$125	$200	$400	$1,000	$2,000	$3,750

Values for notes above $100 are for certified (professionally graded) pieces.

W-8589 • $3 • 139,811 printed. Nature printing: Three-lobed rose leaf. The bird's head on the 1779 issue is differently positioned than on earlier $3 bills.

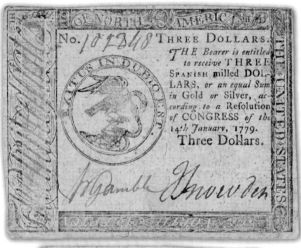

Signed by
William Gamble and J. Snowden.

	VG-8	F-12	VF-20	EF-40	AU-50	Unc-63	Unc-65
2009	$70	$85	$150	$200	$275	$625	$1,250
2020	$100	$125	$150	$300	$750	$1,500	$3,500

Values for notes above $100 are for certified (professionally graded) pieces.

W-8590 • **$4** • 139,811 printed. Nature printing: Mulberry leaf.

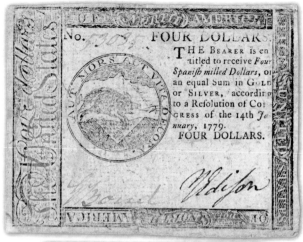

Signed by
George Bond and Thomas Edison.

	VG-8	F-12	VF-20	EF-40	AU-50	Unc-63	Unc-65
2009	$70	$85	$150	$200	$275	$625	$1,250
2020	$100	$125	$150	$300	$750	$1,500	$3,500

Values for notes above $100 are for certified (professionally graded) pieces.

W-8591 • $5 • 139,811 printed. Nature printing: Feverfew leaf. Newman: The letter R in DOLLARS broke in the course of printing and shifted. It was replaced and was no longer higher than the S. The period in the same word was moved to the right. The outside double circle of the emblem was damaged at the lower right. Thus, there are two plate states for this issue.

Signed by
Joseph Gaither and D. Wistar.

	VG-8	F-12	VF-20	EF-40	AU-50	Unc-63	Unc-65
2009	$70	$85	$150	$200	$275	$625	$1,250
2020	$100	$125	$150	$300	$750	$1,500	$3,500

Values for notes above $100 are for certified (professionally graded) pieces.

W-8592 • $20 • 139,811 printed. Nature printing: Grape leaf.

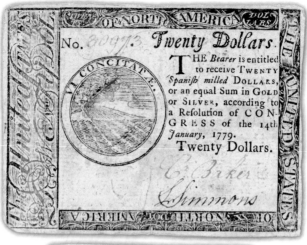

**Signed by
C. Baker and L. Simmons.**

	VG-8	F-12	VF-20	EF-40	AU-50	Unc-63	Unc-65
2009	$70	$85	$150	$200	$275	$625	$1,250
2020	$100	$125	$150	$300	$750	$1,500	$3,500

Values for notes above $100 are for certified (professionally graded) pieces.

W-8593 • **$30** • 182,070 printed. Nature printing: Climbing fumitory leaf.

Signed by
James Dundas and John Reed.

	VG-8	F-12	VF-20	EF-40	AU-50	Unc-63	Unc-65
2009	$70	$85	$150	$200	$275	$625	$1,250
2020	$100	$125	$150	$300	$750	$1,500	$3,500

Values for notes above $100 are for certified (professionally graded) pieces.

W-8594 • **$35** • 182,070 printed. Nature printing: Two willow leaves oriented in different directions.

Signed by
John Helm and William Gray.

	VG-8	F-12	VF-20	EF-40	AU-50	Unc-63	Unc-65
2009	$90	$115	$200	$275	$375	$750	$1,500
2020	$100	$125	$150	$350	$1,000	$2,000	$3,750

Values for notes above $100 are for certified (professionally graded) pieces.

W-8595 • **$40** • 182,070 printed. Nature printing: Poterium leaf and two smaller different leaves.

Signed by
William Gamble and J. Snowden.

	VG-8	F-12	VF-20	EF-40	AU-50	Unc-63	Unc-65
2009	$70	$85	$150	$200	$275	$625	$1,250
2020	$100	$125	$150	$300	$750	$1,500	$3,500

Values for notes above $100 are for certified (professionally graded) pieces.

W-8596 • $45 • 182,070 printed. Nature printing: Ground ivy twig with leaves.

Signed by
Robert Roberts and Samuel Lyon.

	VG-8	F-12	VF-20	EF-40	AU-50	Unc-63	Unc-65
2009	$90	$115	$200	$275	$375	$750	$1,500
2020	$100	$125	$150	$350	$1,000	$2,000	$3,750

Values for notes above $100 are for certified (professionally graded) pieces.

W-8597 • **$50** • 182,070 printed. Nature printing: Two parsley leaves.

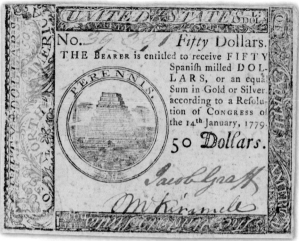

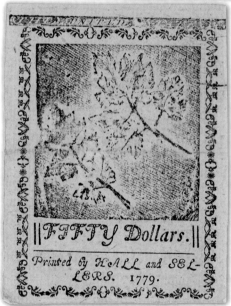

Signed by
Jacob Graff and Michael Kimmell.

	VG-8	F-12	VF-20	EF-40	AU-50	Unc-63	Unc-65
2009	$70	$85	$150	$200	$275	$625	$1,250
2020	$100	$125	$150	$300	$750	$1,500	$3,500

Values for notes above $100 are for certified (professionally graded) pieces.

W-8598 • **$55** • 182,070 printed. Nature printing: Two leaves, the longer one willow.

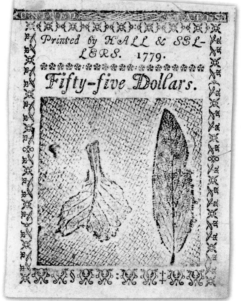

**Signed by
Samuel Nicholas and Isaac Gray.**

	VG-8	F-12	VF-20	EF-40	AU-50	Unc-63	Unc-65
2009	$90	$115	$200	$275	$375	$750	$1,500
2020	$100	$125	$150	$350	$1,000	$2,000	$3,750

Values for notes above $100 are for certified (professionally graded) pieces.

W-8599 • $60 • 182,071 printed. Nature printing: Two leaves. Poison hemlock and willow.

Signed by
James Dundas and John Read.

	VG-8	F-12	VF-20	EF-40	AU-50	Unc-63	Unc-65
2009	$70	$85	$150	$200	$275	$625	$1,250
2020	$100	$125	$150	$300	$750	$1,500	$3,500

Values for notes above $100 are for certified (professionally graded) pieces.

W-8600 • $65 • 182,070 printed. Nature printing: Parsley leaf.

Signed by
John Graff and Jacob Masoner.

	VG-8	F-12	VF-20	EF-40	AU-50	Unc-63	Unc-65
2009	$90	$115	$150	$200	$275	$750	$1,500
2020	$100	$125	$150	$350	$1,000	$2,000	$3,750

Values for notes above $100 are for certified (professionally graded) pieces.

W-8601 • **$70** • 139,811 printed. Nature printing: Maple leaf.

Signed by
John Helm and Isaac Gray.

	VG-8	F-12	VF-20	EF-40	AU-50	Unc-63	Unc-65
2009	$100	$150	$200	$300	$450	$1,000	$2,000
2020	$100	$125	$150	$350	$1,000	$2,000	$4,000

Values for notes above $100 are for certified (professionally graded) pieces.

W-8602 • **$80** • 139,811 printed. Nature printing: Strawberry leaf.

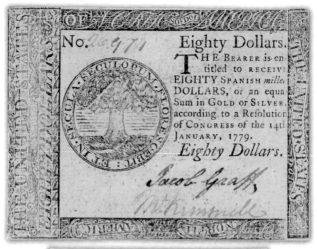

Signed by
Jacob Graff and Michael Kimmell.

	VG-8	F-12	VF-20	EF-40	AU-50	Unc-63	Unc-65
2009	$125	$175	$250	$400	$600	$1,500	$2,500
2020	$125	$150	$250	$600	$1,250	$2,500	$4,500

Values for notes above $100 are for certified (professionally graded) pieces.

COUNTERFEIT CONTINENTAL CURRENCY BILLS

Counterfeiting was a major problem throughout the issuing period of the bills. Counterfeits were made in three main ways:

1. By setting type and making a plate for a bill with type as well as engraved vignettes. Certain of these are extremely sophisticated and differ from the originals only by minor features.

2. By engraving a copper plate in simulation of an original bill. These are differently detailed, as can be noticed when carefully examined, and are not as dangerous as the preceding. Some plates were produced with better details by dampening a bill and pressing it with an iron against the plate, accurately transferring the details to enable more accurate engraving.

3. By using paper and ink to draw a facsimile. Such bills were necessarily produced in small numbers, usually by individuals rather than a group of counterfeiters. Most are crude.

For the various types of counterfeits, signatures were added in ink, sometimes copying original signatures and in other instances with completely fictitious names.

Certain genuine issues were printed on blue paper and distributed to aid in counterfeit detection.

Continental Currency was widely counterfeited in Great Britain and to a lesser extent in continental Europe. These bills were shipped in bulk to the United States and secretly sold to anyone who would buy them. Counterfeiting also took place on board the HMS *Phoenix* anchored off New York City, beginning in January 1776. John and George Foliott began by counterfeiting $30 bills that were secretly sold to Yankee patriot distributors, who spread them widely, obviously a conflict of true patriotism. This continued until at least April 1777.[10] Bills of the states were also counterfeited. This was the first widespread use of counterfeiting as a weapon of war and it pushed the Continental Congress to the brink of insolvency.

In October 1778 John Blair and David Farnsworth, who were part of the Tory distribution network for bogus *Phoenix* bills, were caught by soldiers near the army encampment in Danbury, Connecticut, with over $10,000 in counterfeit Continental Currency on their persons. General George Washington

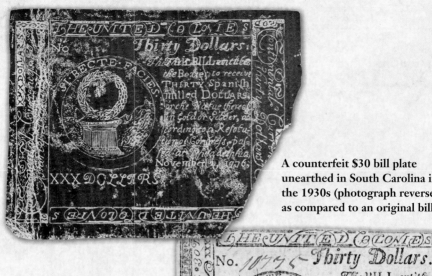

A counterfeit $30 bill plate unearthed in South Carolina in the 1930s (photograph reversed), as compared to an original bill.

A 1776 eighteen-pence note from Burlington, New Jersey, with the inscription "To counterfeit is death."

was informed of the situation and directed that it was "necessary to have them executed," but not before confessions were extracted. The necessary confessions were obtained and the two civilians were tried before a military court-martial, where their primary defense was that they were small-time operators compared to others in the network who were circulating much larger sums. The court-martial panel was unimpressed with their defense and the two were convicted, sentenced to death, and hanged in November 1778.[11]

During their 1776–1783 occupation of New York City the British continued to print large quantities of such bills. The *New York Gazette and Weekly Mercury*, printed in the occupied city on January 20, 1777, included this article that certainly prompted readers to distrust any Continental Currency:

> There has lately been, as we understand by a gentleman just arrived from New England, a large distribution in the country of counterfeited Continental bills so amicably executed as not easily to be discerned from those issued by order of Congress. This has contributed not a little to lower their value and will be one effectual bar to the repayment or liquidation.

The same journal followed with this on March 31:

> In order 'tis supposed, to increase the credit of Continental Currency, a vast number of paper dollars counterfeited in a very masterly manner have been thrown into circulation in several colonies within the course of last fall and winter. Many reams have been brought over by merchants and others and distributed for that purpose.

Even more to the point was this advertisement published in New York City in the *New York Gazette and Weekly Mercury* on April 14, later reprinted elsewhere:

> Persons going into other colonies may be supplied with any number of counterfeit Congress bills for the price of paper per ream. They are so neatly and exactly executed that there is no risqué in getting them off, it being almost impossible to discover that they are not genuine. This has been proved by bills to a very large amount which have already been successfully circulated.
>
> Enquire for Q.E.D. [further information not known] at the Coffee House from 11 P.M. to 4 A.M. during the present month.

On May 20, 1777, the *Maryland Journal* published this:

> Fish-Kill, May 8. Some days ago a villain was taken up at Peek's-Kill in whose custody was found eighty-eight counterfeit Connecticut 40s bills and one of 30 dollars Continental Currency, badly done, being more pale and fainter impressed than the true one; those of Connecticut are done on copper-plate and not easy to be distinguished from the true ones. . . . We likewise hear that another of those adventurers, with £2,700 of counterfeit money about him, is secured at Peek's-Kill. . . .

It was further suggested that the villain had procured the bills in New York City from the aforementioned Q.E.D., whose advertisement was reprinted at the bottom of the news account.

On August 9, 1779, the American frigate *Deane* captured the *Glencairn*, a British ship sailing from Glasgow, Scotland, to New York City. The *Virginia Gazette*, October 2, 1779, told what was discovered:

> On board the *Glencairn* a person says he had in charge a box which was to be delivered to some person in New York, but upon our coming up with them and the ship striking, threw it overboard; upon which we went immediately after it and with difficulty got it before it sunk.
>
> Upon examination we found it contained materials for counterfeiting our currency, consisting of types, paper with silk and isinglass in it, &c. We have however determined to secure the person, as we believe him to be the sole intender of the villainy. The box we have on board and shall bring it with us to Boston.

Counterfeiting proved to be a very effective weapon and had multiple effects, including increasing the distrust of Continental Currency by citizens and forcing Congress to enact legislation recalling certain issues that were extensively copied.[12]

W E, the People of the United States, in order to form a more perfect Union, establish Justice, insure domestic Tranquility, provide for the common Defence, promote the General Welfare, and secure the Blessings of Liberty to Ourselves and our Posterity, do ordain and establish this Constitution for the United States of America.

ARTICLE I.

Sect. 1. ALL legislative powers herein granted shall be vested in a Congress of the United States, which shall consist of a Senate and House of Representatives.

Sect. 2. The House of Representatives shall be composed of members chosen every second year by the people of the several states, and the electors in each state shall have the qualifications requisite for electors of the most numerous branch of the state legislature.

No person shall be a representative who shall not have attained to the age of twenty-five years, and been seven years a citizen of the United States, and who shall not, when elected, be an inhabitant of that state in which he shall be chosen.

Representatives and direct taxes shall be apportioned among the several states which may be included within this Union, according to their respective numbers, which shall be determined by adding to the whole number of free persons, including those bound to service for a term of years, and excluding Indians not taxed, three-fifths of all other persons. The actual enumeration shall be made within three years after the first meeting of the Congress of the United States, and within every subsequent term of ten years, in such manner as they shall by law direct. The number of representatives shall not exceed one for every thirty thousand, but each state shall have at least one representative; and until such enumeration shall be made, the state of New-Hampshire shall be entitled to chuse three, Massachusetts eight, Rhode-Island and Providence Plantations one, Connecticut five, New-York six, New-Jersey four, Pennsylvania eight, Delaware one, Maryland six, Virginia ten, North-Carolina five, South-Carolina five, and Georgia three.

When vacancies happen in the representation from any state, the Executive authority thereof shall issue writs of election to fill such vacancies.

The House of Representatives shall chuse their Speaker and other officers; and shall have the sole power of impeachment.

Sect. 3. The Senate of the United States shall be composed of two senators from each state, chosen by the legislature thereof, for six years; and each senator shall have one vote.

Immediately after they shall be assembled in consequence of the first election, they shall be divided as equally as may be into three classes. The seats of the senators of the first class shall be vacated at the expiration of the second year, of the second class at the expiration of the fourth year, and of the third class at the expiration of the sixth year, so that one-third may be chosen every second year; and if vacancies happen by resignation, or otherwise, during the recess of the Legislature of any state, the Executive thereof may make temporary appointments until the next meeting of the Legislature, which shall then fill such vacancies.

No person shall be a senator who shall not have attained to the age of thirty years, and been nine years a citizen of the United States, and who shall not, when elected, be an inhabitant of that state for which he shall be chosen.

The Vice-President of the United States shall be President of the senate, but shall have no vote, unless they be equally divided.

The senate shall chuse their other officers, and also a President pro tempore, in the absence of the Vice-President, or when he shall exercise the office of President of the United States.

The Senate shall have the sole power to try all impeachments. When sitting for that purpose, they shall be on oath or affirmation. When the President of the United States is tried, the Chief Justice shall preside: And no person shall be convicted without the concurrence of two-thirds of the members present.

Judgment in cases of impeachment shall not extend further than to removal from office, and disqualification to hold and enjoy any office of honor, trust or profit under the United States: but the party convicted shall nevertheless be liable and subject to indictment, trial, judgment and punishment, according to law.

Sect. 4. The times, places and manner of holding elections for senators and representatives, shall be prescribed in each state by the legislature thereof; but the Congress may at any time by law make or alter such regulations, except as to the places of chusing Senators.

The Congress shall assemble at least once in every year, and such meeting shall be on the first Monday in December, unless they shall by law appoint a different day.

Sect. 5. Each house shall be the judge of the elections, returns and qualifications of its own members, and a majority of each shall constitute a quorum to do business; but a smaller number may adjourn from day to day, and may be authorized to compel the attendance of absent members, in such manner, and under such penalties as each house may provide.

Each house may determine the rules of its proceedings, punish its members for disorderly behaviour, and, with the concurrence of two-thirds, expel a member.

Each house shall keep a journal of its proceedings, and from time to time publish the same, excepting such parts as may in their judgment require secrecy; and the yeas and nays of the members of either house on any question shall, at the desire of one-fifth of those present, be entered on the journal.

Neither house, during the session of Congress, shall, without the consent of the other, adjourn for more than three days, nor to any other place than that in which the two houses shall be sitting.

Sect. 6. The senators and representatives shall receive a compensation for their services, to be ascertained by law, and paid out of the treasury of the United States. They shall in all cases, except treason, felony and breach of the peace, be privileged from arrest during their attendance at the session of their respective houses, and in going to and returning from the same; and for any speech or debate in either house, they shall not be questioned in any other place.

No senator or representative shall, during the time for which he was elected, be appointed to any civil office under the authority of the United States, which shall have been created, or the emoluments whereof shall have been encreased during such time; and no person holding any office under the United States, shall be a member of either house during his continuance in office.

Sect. 7. All bills for raising revenue shall originate in the house of representatives; but the senate may propose or concur with amendments as on other bills.

Every bill which shall have passed the house of representatives and the senate, shall, before it become a law, be presented to the president of the United States; if he approve he shall sign it, but if not he shall return it, with his objections to that house in which it shall have originated, who shall enter the objections at large on their journal, and proceed to reconsider it. If after such reconsideration two-thirds of that house shall agree to pass the bill, it shall be sent, together with the objections, to the other house, by which it shall likewise be reconsidered, and if approved by two-thirds of that house, it shall become a law. But in all such cases the votes of both houses shall

4

Selected Contemporary Citations

———————❧———————

News about Continental Currency was continually printed in American papers. Human rights and free speech were violated when it became a criminal offense to state anything negative about the currency, including when the bills depreciated sharply in value. Many citizens were imprisoned—not different from what a totalitarian or dictatorial government would do. This aspect of American history has been generally omitted from popular texts. Among the detailed early texts with information about the government's abuse of citizens are *Political Essays on the Nature and Operation of Money, Public Finances, and Other Subjects: Published during the American War and continued up to the present year 1791*, by Pelatiah Webster, which also tells of his imprisonment and loss of most of his possessions when the British occupied New York City (1776 to 1783), and *Historical Sketch of Continental Paper Money*, by Samuel Breck, 1863, which gives extensive details, including citations not in Webster.

In contrast, during the Revolutionary War there were countless articles about the depreciation of Continental Currency printed in the British press and also published in New York City during the occupation. Estimates of the degree of depreciation at any given time varied widely, not only as published by the British but also by historians in later years.

CITATIONS

June 26, 1775. *Hartford* (Connecticut) *Courant*:

> The following resolutions are reported to have passed in the Continental Congress at Philadelphia, viz. immediately to strike a continental currency of two millions of dollars. To raise 15,000 more men, 5,000 of whom to be stationed at New York. That Col. Washington was appointed commander in chief of the American forces and was going to Boston with 1,000 rifle men.

July 7, 1775. *North-Carolina Weekly Gazette* (New Bern):

> By letters from the Congress of the 19th of June we are informed that Col. Washington, of Virginia, is appointed commander in chief of all American forces. General Ward of Massachusetts and General Lee to be major generals; Major Gates of Virginia to be adjutant general with the rank of brigadier. That 15,000 troops are voted to be in pay of the Continent, 10,000 for Boston and 5,000 for New York. The New England colonies have voted 22,000 for their service, to that 7,000 will be a weight on themselves. Col. Philip Schuyler to be second in command of the New York forces. That a sum of money equal to two millions of dollars is to be struck to be a Continental Currency and sunk in seven years by a tax on the provinces in proportion to their respective number of inhabitants . . .

George Washington is appointed commander-in-chief by the Continental Congress.

January 15, 1776. *Pennsylvania Packet* (Philadelphia):

In Committee, Dover, January 4, 1776.

Resolved, That the keeping up the credit of the Continental Currency is essential to support the United Colonies in their virtuous opposition to ministerial oppression; and that the refusing to take said currency in payment of debts, &c. will tend to depreciate the value of the same.

Resolved, That it appears to this committee by the confession of John Cowgill, a resident of Little Creek Hundred, in this county, that he has refused and from conscience shall refuse to take said Continental money in discharge of debts or for other purposes when tendered to him.

Therefore *unanimously Resolved,* That it is the opinion of the committee that the aforesaid John Cowgill is, by such his conduct, an enemy to his country and ought to be treated as such by every friend to American liberty—And that they ought to have no further dealings with him.

Thomas Rodney, chairman.

February 4, 1776. *Pennsylvania Gazette* (Philadelphia). Review of court proceedings, including these excerpts:

Whereas the Continental Congress die lately resolve. "That if any person should be so lost to all virtue and regard for this country as to refuse to receive the bills of credit issued by the authority of Congress or should obstruct or discourage the currency thereof, and be convicted by the committee of the city, country, or district where he should reside, such person should be deemed, published, and treated as an enemy of his country and be precluded from all trade or intercourse with the inhabitants of these colonies."

And, whereas John Drinker, hatter, Thomas and Samuel Fisher of the house of Joshua Fisher and Sons, merchants, all of this city, having been charged with a breach of this resolve, in refusing to receive the above bills of credit in payment, appeared before this committee, acknowledged the truth of the charge, and alleged in their defense scruples of conscience thereupon, as being money emitted for the purposes of war.

The committee stated that Congress made no exceptions, and that their plea was involved. Further, the defendants regularly accepted currency issued by the various colonies, some of which was used for war and defense. Accordingly, they were prohibited from doing any further business. In the same session other citizens were also found guilty.

March 17, 1776. *Hartford Courant*:

The constables and collectors of the Colony taxes are hereby informed that Continental Currency will be received by the treasurer of the Colony of Connecticut in all payments in the Treasury.

Treasury Office, 12th March, 1776

April 1, 1776. *Hartford Courant*:

Lost last Friday between Ely Warner's in Suffield and Elijah Alderman's in Simsbury a leather pocket book, almost new, containing two four dollar bills and one three dollar bill Continental Currency, and two notes of hand, one for twelve pounds, the other two pounds eleven shillings. Whoever has found said pocket book and will send it to the printer or Capt. Veits in Turkey-Hills shall have two dollars reward.

March 18, 1776

April 2, 1776. *Hartford Courant*:

We hear that the Continental Currency is received in payment and passes very freely among the inhabitants of the French West Indian Islands.

May 18, 1776. *Jackson's Oxford Journal* (Oxford, Oxfordshire, England):

In the month of January last a trader at New York imported a cargo from the West Indies, which he expected would have turned out to good account, but when the money came due he was offered Continental paper Currency.

Not approving it he demanded a return of his goods, which was refused, and he was taken before some self-created rulers who gave him his choice to take the Currency or to be sent for a soldier. Refusing still to take it, he was accordingly sent to serve at Massachusetts Bay; but though he did not like his situation he was more disgusted at his officers, the captain of the company being a tripeman, the lieutenants a box maker and a jobbing farrier, and the ensign a convict from England who had been on his travels for about four years. The injured trader therefore took the first opportunity to desert, got to Boston, and embarked on board the fleet when they left that place.

May 29, 1776. *The Pennsylvania Packet* (Philadelphia):

Extract of a letter from New York dated May 13. Friday last information was given to our Congress that some men near Coal Spring on Long Island were counterfeiting Continental Currency. A party of militia were ordered out in the afternoon in search of them. They are all taken with what cash they had struck off and their tools. They are expected in town this day, and hope they will be provided with a halter or sent to the Simsbury mines.

John Dunlap owned and printed the *Pennsylvania Packet*, which reported weekly on the war against the British and patriotic interests, including Continental Currency. His press was also put to work in July 1776 to print the first published copies of the Declaration of Independence, called "Dunlap broadsides," and in 1787 he printed copies of the Constitution for the Constitutional Convention.

November 14, 1776. *The Maryland Gazette* (Annapolis):

We hear that on the evacuation of our fortresses on Long Island the Continental Currency sunk in its value one thousand per cent, but that now it has gained its nominal value and passes currently among the British troops and Tories as well as among our friends; what was the occasion of this strange turn is a matter of much speculation.

January 4, 1777. *The Pennsylvania Packet* (Philadelphia):

In Congress, December 17, 1776.

Resolved, That the Council of Safety of Pennsylvania be requested to take the most vigorous and speedy measures tor punishing all such as shall refuse Continental Currency, and that the general be directed to give all necessary aid to the Council of Safety for carrying their measures on this subject into effectual execution.

By order of Congress,
John Hancock, president

Baltimore, Dec. 27, 1776

Gentlemen,

The great importance of the welfare of these United States of supporting the credit of the Continental Currency will suggest the propriety of the above resolve which I am commanded by Congress to transmit t[o] you, and request you will take measures for an immediate compliance therewith.

I have wrote to the general to give you every necessary assistance in carrying your determinations on this subject into effectual execution.

I have the honor to be, Gentlemen, Your most humble servant,

John Hancock, president
Council of Safety, Philadelphia

January 1, 1777

In consequence of the foregoing resolve of Congress and the intelligence received from several parts of this state, that the disaffected and enemies to the United States of America are pursuing the most dangerous schemes to destroy the credit of the money issued under the authority of Congress, which wicked and mischievous practices are likely to be attended with the most pernicious consequences, unless immediately suppressed by a speedy and vigorous exertion of the powers invested in this council. Therefore

Resolved, that if any person or persons from and after the publication of this resolve shall refuse to take Continental Currency in payment of any debt or contract whatsoever, or for any goods, merchandise, or commodity offered for sale, or shall ask a greater price for any such commodity in Continental Currency than in any other kind of money or specie, on full proof made thereof before any three members of any county committee, or any three field officers of militia of this state, the person or persons so offending shall for the first offense be considered as a dangerous member of society, and forfeit the goods offered for sale or bargained for, or from whom such debt is due. And shall moreover pay a fine of five pounds to the state, to be levied immediately by the persons to whom forfeitures are directed to be paid by this resolve, provided such debt or contract do not exceed that sum. But if the debt due or price of such goods bargained for or offered for sale exceed the sum of five pounds, then the person offending as aforesaid shall, besides the debt due, goods contracted for or offered for sale, forfeit to the full amount of said debt, contract or price agreed on or demanded, one third part of such forfeiture to the use of the informer and the remaining two thirds to this state, to be paid to the committee of the county where the forfeiture is incurred, or where no such committee exists, to the three field officers of the next nearest battalion, or by them transmitted to the public treasury of this state, after deducting reasonable costs, such forfeiture to be levied immediately by the directors and authority of the said committee or field officers. And every person so offending shall for the second offense be subjected to the aforementioned penalties and be banished [from] this state, to such place and in such manner as this council shall direct.

Nevertheless, if any person shall think himself or herself aggrieved by the determination of any of the said committees or field officers, he or she shall be allowed to appeal to this council, provided that the said appeal be made within six weeks after such determination made and information given by the said committees or field officers to the parties in writing—A regular record of the proceedings in every case to be transmitted to this board in four weeks after determination.

Resolved, That all persons whose shops, stores or warehouses have heretofore been shut up and have been restrained from carrying on commercial intercourse with the inhabitants of this state for refusing Continental Currency shall be released from such restraint and permitted to open their shops, stores and warehouses, and that all persons who are in confinement for the same offense be immediately discharged from such confinement, to be subject nevertheless to the penalties described in the foregoing resolution for future offenses.

By order of the Council,

Thomas Wharton, Jun., President

January 30, 1777. Resolution of the Council of Safety, Philadelphia:

The Council of Safety at Philadelphia, in compliance with a resolve of the Continental Congress, are taking the most vigorous and speedy measures for punishing all such as shall refuse Continental Currency.

By a declaration of the Continental Congress, published before they left Philadelphia, all goods are positively declared to be forfeited for which the paper currency of the United States is refused in payment.

February 18, 1777. *The Pennsylvania Packet* (Philadelphia):

We hear from Connecticut that a pint of salt has been sold for 3d lawful money, but it must be observed that the consideration was paid in Continental Currency—An irrefragable proof as well of the immense scarcity of salt as of the incredible depreciation of the dirty trash that was bartered away for it.

April 8, 1777. *Maryland Journal* (Baltimore):

Philadelphia, April 2

A gentleman of the first rank in this city has received a letter from his correspondent in France, who is one of the most eminent merchants in that kingdom, informing him that the commercial interest in that country were so much in favour of the gallant English Americans that, under sanction of the government, they had begun and hoped soon to establish a bank in favour of Continental Currency, and did not doubt by all the powers in Europe would immediately receive it, except the English, whose distressed finances, it was expected, would soon oblige them to acknowledge the Americans to be free and independent states.

May 5, 1778. *Dunlap's Maryland Gazette* (Baltimore):

To be sold, a parcel of valuable country-born slaves, for Continental Currency, by the subscriber living in Calvert County. April 20th. John Weems, Junior.

January 25, 1779. *Boston Gazette*:

Much of late has been said respecting our present circulating currency, by persons I conceive are afraid of losing a little of its nominal value. As the press is free and the opinion of many are given, permit a soldier, who before he became such, was possessed of a sufficiency, but at present not possessed of much, to offer some remarks.

Persons who have been trading the whole of this war, who have purchased sundry estates which neither they nor their progeny, had it not taken place could have thought of (I have reference to all those petty engrossers, retailers & traders who have never ventured one shilling to characterize them as merchants) I say such a set of the community, hearing that cash will, or fearing its depreciation, is troubled day and night about the chance of losing perhaps a twentieth part of what their oppression as amassed them; this being the case they fly to write in the newspapers; would they appear unmasked the world would be a better judge of their designs. There is little occasion I take it for granted, to use much argument on this point, the community at large must be satisfied those productions result from persons deeply dipped in avarice or so possessed of overgrown fortunes mostly got by unfair dealing.

An illustration of colonial Baltimore.

The narrative continues, blaming merchants for raising prices and not realizing that it was the depreciation of the currency that caused the problem. Later in the letter the writer comments:

I would propose the following queries:

1st. Ought a soldier to be paid in the Continental currency at its present depreciation the same wages he received three years ago and no more?

2nd. Should he suffer the losses already incurred?

3rd. Will he not be pennyless at the expiration of his enlistment?

4th. Is it possible to conceive that the merchant can expect his cash made equal to gold and silver before the army has been redressed? Will not all the hardships, fatigues, losses, and hazards entitle him to be on a par at least with these gentlemen?

My affections are facts, and may my last observations I hope will be taken notice of. . . .

The honorable legislative body in their wisdom thought wages or allowances made three or four years ago was inadequate, and their wonted consideration raised their, which I affirm was a real necessity, they likewise passed an act making fees three time as much as formerly. . . .

From month to month things grow daily worse, so much that at last we find many instances of poverty in rags and other deeply in debt. . . .

I hope the longest sufferers will be the first attended to, and I have reason to hope that the contempt a set of those men shows to the soldiers at this day will be otherwise noticed by the legislative authority, that to cast by all their services, losses, and dangers, for the securing of a set of monopolizers in their ill got pelf.

A SOLDIER.

January 28, 1779. *Pennsylvania Journal* (Philadelphia):

To be sold in Chester Town, Maryland, the house and lot on which the subscriber now dwells. . . . The whole to be sold for sterling bills, gold, or Continental Currency of the emission of May 20, 1777, or April 11, 1778, by William Geddes.[1]

February 8, 1779, *Boston Gazette*:

To be sold for Continental Currency of the emission of May 20, 1777, or April 11, 1778.

One hundred acres of unimproved land in the southeasterly part of Lancaster, formerly own'd by Jonas Powers. For further particulars inquire of the subscriber at Marlborough. Wm. Palfrey

Marlboro', Jan. 23, 1779

May 20, 1779. *The Pennsylvania Packet* (Philadelphia):

At a court of oyer and terminer [a particular type of court] held in Dutchess County, State of New York, Isaac Youngs and William Jaycocks were capitally convicted, the former for horse stealing and the latter for bringing counterfeit money from the enemy. This last offense being of the most pernicious tendency was made capital by a late act of that Legislature, whereby it is declared that whosoever shall bring any counterfeit bills of credit emitted by Congress or that state or any of the United States within the power of the enemy, knowing them to be counterfeit, shall suffer death. The above criminals were executed on the 22nd of April last.

November 22, 1779. *The Pennsylvania Packet* (Philadelphia):

At a court of oyer and terminer held at York Town for the county of York, commencing the 11th of October 1779, before the Honorable Thomas McKean and William Augustus Atlee, Esquires, Nathaniel Patton and Henry Trout were convicted and condemned to be hanged for passing counterfeit 30 dollar bills of Continental money of the emissions of 22nd July 1776, knowing it to be counterfeit . . .

George Werle, Christian Bixler, Michael Werle, and Christian Hooper were tried and convicted of passing counterfeit 40 dollar bills of the emission of April 1788, and praying the benefit of clergy, were burnt in the brawn of the left thumb with a letter.

November 23, 1779. *The Pennsylvania Packet* (Philadelphia):

Mark Millekin was convicted of having stamps in his possession, with intent to counterfeit Continental 40 dollar bills of the 11th April 1778, and to impose such counterfeits on the good people of the state as genuine bills. He was sentenced to the pillory for one year, to pay a fine of £2,000, for his good behavior, and that he shall keep the peace to all the liege people of this Commonwealth during the present war.

Philadelphia was home to the
Continental Congress
for much of 1776.

Part II

~

1776
Continental
Dollars

1776 Continental dollar, variety with CURENCY spelling.

5
History and Aspects of Continental Dollars

FIRST FEDERAL COINS?

One of the most significant early American issues is the so-called Continental dollar. Bearing devices and inscriptions taken from Continental Currency paper money (of the authorization of February 17, 1776), these feature on the obverse the 1776 date and, surrounding the inscription, CONTINENTAL CURRENCY. Within is a sundial, below which is MIND YOUR BUSINESS, with FUGIO (from the Roman *tempus fugit*, or "time flies") to the left. The reverse displays 13 intertwined circles, each with the name or abbreviation of a state, joined to form a linked chain border. Within the center is the inscription AMERICAN CONGRESS WE ARE ONE.

No specific contemporary documentation has been found regarding the origin of a metallic (rather than paper) Continental Currency piece. The resolution of February 1776, pertaining to the issuance of paper money, resulted in the production of different denominations from the 1/6 dollar through $8, including the $1 denomination. The resolution of May 9, 1776, provided for various denominations from $1 through $8. However, the resolution of July 22, 1776, significantly omitted the $1 and contained denominations from $2 through $30. Likewise, the final resolution of that year, November 2, 1776, omitted the $1 bill and began with the $2.

Several different die varieties were made. *Currency* was spelled three ways: CURRENCY, CURENCY, and CURRENCEY, the last being imitative of an error found on the 1/6 dollar bill of February 17, 1776, suggesting that the engraver may have copied the specific legends on this particular design while making the dies. The typical pewter strike is about 41 mm in diameter; the edge is ornamented with twin olive leaves in the manner of Spanish-American dollars (8-reales coins) of the era, although there are variants. Perhaps a relevant connection: Continental Currency paper dollars were to be redeemable in these Spanish coins.

Most Continental dollars are described as being made of pewter, and elemental analysis has revealed that typical examples are 83 to 93 percent tin with the balance being mostly lead.[1] The definition of pewter has varied over the years, but pewter is still the appropriate term for Continental dollars. Weights vary, with most being in the range of 245 to 275 grains against a standard of 255 grains, although the range reported by John M. Kleeberg is from 210 to 305 grains.[2] This indicates that the planchets were hand trimmed and not punched from a sheet. Obviously, this was a labor-intensive process.

An embarkation of Continental soldiers in New London, Connecticut, in 1776, the year that the Continental dollar was presumably created.

THE MINTING AND DISTRIBUTION MYSTERY

A commentary by Michael J. Hodder, cataloger of the John J. Ford Jr. Collection catalog (Stack's, Part I, October 2003), includes this:

> It is almost certain that the first 1776 Continental dollars were struck in New York City in the summer of 1776, just before the British captured the city in September. This fits with Ford's observation that New York state omitted the $1 denomination from the currency issue of August 13.

The *New-York Journal*, June 27, 1776, printed this rumor:

> We hear it proposed, that after three months, the currency of all Copper Coin made of bad metal, or wanting in weight, is to pass at the rate of 15 for an eighth part of a dollar. And if it shall appear that there is not a sufficiency for common use, that it will be all called in, and a new impression struck of Continental Copper Coin, of a larger size; twelve of which is to pass for an eighth of a dollar, after which no other coppers are to pass current.

No such copper coinage is known to have been made, however, and it is likely that this has no connection with the Continental dollars. Further, from the Hodder narrative:

> The New York mint may not have had enough time to strike all the 1776 Continental dollars before the British captured the city. The coiners probably packed what they could and smuggled themselves and whatever machinery they could conveniently carry out of the city just before it fell to the enemy. Since the coinage was official Continental Congress business, the

New York in 1776.

mint traveled with the Congress wherever it went. The second group of Continental dollars was struck after the Mint left New York, when the Congress settled in Pennsylvania. Philadelphia and Lancaster have been proposed as mint sites for the E.G. FECIT, CURRENCY, and floral cross varieties. . . .

The *London Chronicle*, December 21, 1776, included this:

> The Congress have established a Mint at Philadelphia, where they coin copper and silver pieces about the size of a half crown. In silver go for twelve shillings, in copper for fourteen pence.[3]

No other information has been learned about this mint and its coins. This has furnished the opportunity for many theories over a long span of years.

For many years it has been a question as to whether Continental dollars circulated as money in the United States. Pierre Eugène Du Simitière, who formed an impressive collection of coins and tokens including colonial and early American issues in the 1770s and 1780s, did not possess an example by the time his collecting seems to have ended in 1783. Du Simitière planned to issue *Common Place Book, 1775–1784*, illustrated by "Medals, Seals, Coins, Devices, Statues, Monuments, Badges, &c . . ." No. 18: "A coin of the Size of a Crown, with devices and Mottos taken from the continental money, Struck't in London on Type-Metal, and dated 1776."[4]

This would indicate that he may have at least seen an example or corresponded concerning the pieces.

Similarly, no contemporary account has been found of any other American collection of the era having such pieces. And there is no record of any having been unearthed by detectorists with electronic metal detectors. In contrast, multiple examples of other early coins have been found this way, including of the very rare 1659 Maryland denarium.

In the late eighteenth century one of America's pioneer numismatists, William Bentley, D.D., of Salem, Massachusetts, entered in his diary some interesting observations of coins he had seen, including this on September 15, 1791:

> Watson, in the fourth volume of his *Chymestry*, has the following: "It is reported of King James II, that he melted down and coined all the brass guns in Ireland and afterwards proceeded to coin the pewter with this inscription, Melioris Lessera Fati." The Congress in America had recoursed the same expedient; they coined several pieces of about an inch and a half

in diameter, and of 240 grains in weight on one side of which was a circular ring near the edge, Continental Currency, 1776, and within the ring a rising sun with Fugio at the side of it, shining upon a dial under which was Mind Your Business. On the reverse were 13 small circles joined together like the rings of a chain, on each of which was inscribed the name of some one of the 13 states. . . .

I have been particular in the mention of this piece of money because, like the leaden money which was struck at Vienna when that city was besieged in 1529, it will soon become a great curiosity. I have estimated the weight of a cubic foot of this Continental Currency. It weighs 7,440 ounces. This exceeds the weight of a cubic foot of our best sort of pewter, and falls short of that of our worst. I conjecture that the metal of this Continental Currency consisted of 12 parts of tin and one of lead.

Presumably, Bentley had viewed or even owned one, perhaps obtained from England, where Watson's information had been published.

Paul Revere, the Boston engraver and metalsmith, wrote this letter to Watson on February 21, 1790 (original spelling preserved):

In perusing your invaluable Essays on Chemistry vol. 4 page 136, you make mention of pewter money coined by the American Congress, and give a description of it. The very great pleasure which I have received from the perusal of those volumes and the very great exceeding good character I have I have heard of you, from some of your countrymen, as a Man, and for fear some person of more consequence, has not endeavoured to set you right in that piece of History;

I have inclosed you two pieces of money, one of them was printed under the direction of the American Congress, the other I am not so fully asured off; as they both answer to your description, except the mettal, I have sent them, supposing, if you were not possessed of them before, they might be acceptable to you as curiosities.

As for pewter money struck in America, I never saw any, and I have made carefull enquiry, and have all the reason in the world to believe, that you were imposed upon by those who informed you.

I am sir with respect & esteem,

Your most hum. servt.

Paul Revere[5]

Especially relevant is Revere's statement that he had never seen a Continental dollar and that careful enquiry had not produced any information as well.

Enter Sarah Sophia Banks (1774–1818), a London lady (and sister and collaborator of famed botanist Sir Joseph Banks) who by 1815 had assembled seven ledgers of things of interest to her.[6] A numismatist par excellence, she

Paul Revere.

had about 8,500 items in her cabinet. The British Museum has the ledgers today, including one with this printed notice attached to a page:

These American MEDALS at

Six-Pence Each.

N.B. Representing the Paper Currency of a Dollar, which goes for Four Shillings and Six-pence in that Country.

EXPLANATION

The Thirteen Colonies united like a Chain, with the Names of each on the Ringlets, the Words, "AMERICAN CONGRESS" within, in the Center, "WE ARE ONE" and with Rays of the Sun shooting to each Ringlet, as a Glory.

The Reverse is the Sun going round its Orbit, with a Motto "FUGIO" signifying, I fly: under the Dial is "MIND YOUR BUSINESS. The Date, 1776, is the time they declared Independency. The Letters E.G, FECIT, its maker's Name.

Given the foregoing, Banks made a notation in her ledger: "Congress Dollar. 1776. Never current; struck on speculation in Europe for sale in America." As no evidence has been found of their circulation on our side of the Atlantic, "struck in Europe" may or may not be true.

Alexandre Vattemare, who visited America on two occasions in the early nineteenth century, studied American coins and, probably based on interviews, stated:

Dollar project[ed]. 1776. Reverse: in a circle composed of thirteen intertwined rings, each bearing the name of one of the thirteen founding states, another circle containing the words: We are one (we are one). This dollar, whose composition is attributed to Franklin, has not been put into circulation.

Vattemare seems to have been the first to disqualify the Continental dollar as a circulating American issue.

In the *American Numismatical Manual*, 1859, Montroville W. Dickeson wrote:

By whomever designed, this coin or medal unburdened the patriotic genius of someone, and it was eminently worthy of the glorious period whose date it bears. It was in itself a treatise, in the then condition of our country, in behalf of liberty; and contrasted now with the more artistic, but much less vigorous, designs upon the present coinage of our national mint, is worthy of imitation.

Our forefathers neglected no opportunity which offered for stimulating the patriotism of the people; for their coins and paper money bore emblems and mottoes calculated to inspire love of country and love of liberty in the everyday relations of both business and pleasure, of which money was, as now, the medium.

With all our admiration for this coin or medal, we have not been able to determine that it was designed for, or that it became to any great extent, a currency. As it made its appearance only in white metal, the idea is strengthened thereby that it was in reality a medal, struck off to commemorate the bold, fearless, and patriotic acts of the Congress that declared our country a free and independent nation.

In 2012 researcher Andrea Grimason was quoted in the *E-Sylum*, the digital publication of the Numismatic Bibliomania Society, expressing skepticism at longstanding numismatic understanding of the Continental dollar: "According to Mr. Newman . . . Benjamin Franklin designed the original Continental Currency coin and in 1776 Elisha Gallaudet redesigned it seven times . . . struck over six thousand coins . . . in three types of metal . . . with three different spellings . . . in two sizes . . . in less than six months . . . in a country that didn't have a mint . . . without anyone knowing."

Following up on that, in the October 21, 2012, edition of the *E-Sylum* numismatic historian Robert D. Leonard contributed "On the Origin of the Continental Dollar." He gave excerpts from "The Congratulation, A Poem," published in the *Nova-Scotia Gazette & Weekly Chronicle* for January 4, 1780 (and before that, in the *Royal Gazette* in New York City, November 6, 1779):

THE CONGRATULATION, A POEM.

Joy to great Congress, joy an hundred fold, The grand cajolers are themselves cajoled . . .

Whoever these important points explains, Congress will nobly pay him for his pains Of pewter dollars what both hands can hold, A thimble-full of plate, a mite of gold . . .

Leonard observed: "It is difficult to read this as anything other than a reference to pewter dollars issued by the (American) Congress no later than 1779 . . . Also, it is possible that researchers have been looking in the wrong year for evidence of the Continental dollars. We are so used to U.S. coins being minted in the year they are dated that we forget about things like the Pine Tree shillings, dated instead to the year of authorization. Perhaps the [emission] of pewter dollars took place as late as 1778 or 1779, with the date of 1776 used in honor of the Declaration of Independence."

Eric P. Newman and Maureen Levine, in "18th Century Writings on the Continental Currency Dollar Coin," in *The Numismatist*, July 2014, gave further stanzas and an extensively detailed biography of Jonathan Odell, writer of the aforementioned poem, and noted that he was a British spy and publicist. They also shared notices about the Continental dollar published in Europe as early as 1783, and later.

In "Shady Stories for U.S. Coins," published in *Coin World* on September 24, 2015, Bill Eckberg discussed numismatic references to the dollar coins published from 1952 onward and reiterated that there were unsolved mysteries concerning their mintage and distribution.

To volume no. 1, issue 2, of the *Journal of Early American Numismatics*, December 2018, John M. Kleeberg contributed "The Continental Dollar; British Medals or American Coins?" The following was included:

> In 1776 New York fell to the British very quickly. Hugh Gaine speedily left the city; his work colleague Elisha Gallaudet probably did as well. There was no time to heft and ferry across to New Jersey heavy kegs filled with freshly struck pewter Continental dollars. So these pristine pieces fell into British Hands.
>
> When the time came to leave New York in 1781–1783 the British grabbed anything that was not nailed down to take home with them as "souvenirs." If nothing else, kegs of Continental dollars would serve as good ballast for the ships, like the counterfeit halfpence that soon would be regularly shipped in the opposite direction.
>
> This explains why Continental dollars became so common in Britain. . . .
>
> The Continental dollars were minted somewhere in or around New York City After the capture of the city most of the supply fell into British (and Hessian) hands. New York City was cut off from the rest of the United States—thus neither Paul Revere nor Pierre du Simitière saw any before 1793. Because the Continental dollars that emerged again after 1783 and later came from British-controlled territory, the false assumption was made that they originated from London.

These seem to be medals rather than legal-tender coins, but as most show evidence of circulation they may have passed in commerce in Europe. If that was the case, the pewter metal may have caused them to be valued less than a silver coin would have been. Facts are elusive. Some thoughts:

1. The design is copied from Continental Currency bills of 1776.
2. As of 2020, none of these coins have been found in the United States by treasure detectorists using electronic equipment.
3. Although Sarah Sophia Banks suggested these were struck in Europe for sale in America, no information has been found concerning any such sales in America.
4. That they were first illustrated and publicized in Europe in the 1780s does not necessarily give credence to the scenario of their being shipped from New York City to England during the Revolution. The pieces were not released in the United States.
5. The identity of E.G. is unknown. Suggestions that the initials may be for Elbridge Gerry (American political figure) or Elisha Gallaudet (American engraver) are not conclusively backed by facts.

For a study of how the *Guide Book of United States Coins* has reported on scholarly understanding of the Continental dollars since 1946, see appendix D.

Kenneth Bressett, editor emeritus of the *Guide Book*, wrote in an email to Whitman publisher Dennis Tucker in May 2020: "One must still question why such finely made pieces would have been made from so many dies, and in different metals, for sale as novelty items and at an extremely low price (as some have suggested). Logic dictates that they were more likely made in Europe (where necessary equipment was available) as a proposed coinage with the intent of obtaining a contract for making coins to fill a need in America. A simple test of the tin content in these pieces might tell if it came from Cornwall."

Such controversies and mysteries over the years contribute to the rich fabric of numismatics. I only need to mention John J. Ford's marvelous discoveries of previously unknown (for a reason) Gold Rush gold coins and ingots, Walter Breen's concoction of "midnight minters" making rarities at the Mint (since debunked), druggist Robert Coulton Davis allegedly supplying laudanum to Mint officials in exchange for rarities (when opiates at the time actually could be purchased easily over the counter, and without prescriptions), and the (supposedly very rare) 1844 Orphan Annie dime. These and other stories caused debate in numismatic circles but are now resolved. We still do not know how and why the 1794 Sheldon-48 Starred Reverse cent was created.

In time, perhaps some *contemporary* (1776) documentation of the 1776 Continental dollar will be found.

MARKET ASPECTS

See chapter 6 for diagnostics and other information on varieties of Continental dollars. Specimens of the Continental dollar struck in pewter, while elusive, do appear on the market with regularity, indicating that the original coinage must have been extensive. A few brass and silver examples are extant and exceedingly rare. Attributions are to Eric P. Newman, "The 1776 Continental Currency Coinage," published in *The Coin Collector's Journal* in 1952. A notable auction offering of these was in the Ford Collection in 2003.

A session of the first Continental Congress, 1774.

6

Continental Dollar Varieties

*T*here are four known obverse and two known reverse dies for Continental dollars. The first study by numbered die varieties was by Eric P. Newman, published in 1952. Newman numbers are the designations most used today, so they precede the following listings. The most detailed study of the dies and their characteristics was by Michael Hodder, "The Continental Currency Coinage of 1776: A Trial Die and Metallic Emission Sequence," published in *The American Numismatic Association Centennial Anthology* in 1991. Extensive citations from this study, lightly edited, are given below. Whitman numbers and pricing in this chapter come from the *Whitman Encyclopedia of Colonial and Early American Coins*.

These listings use the Universal Rarity Scale (URS) below to indicate the availability of each variety.

URS-0	None known	URS-11	500 to 999
URS-1	1 known, unique	URS-12	1,000 to 1,999
URS-2	2 known	URS-13	2,000 to 3,999
URS-3	3 or 4	URS-14	4,000 to 7,999
URS-4	5 to 8	URS-15	8,000 to 15,999
URS-5	9 to 16	URS-16	16,000 to 31,999
URS-6	17 to 32	URS-17	32,000 to 64,999
URS-7	33 to 64	URS-18	65,000 to 124,999
URS-8	65 to 124	URS-19	125,000 to 249,999
URS-9	125 to 249	URS-20	250,000 to 499,999
URS-10	250 to 499	URS-21	500,000 to 999,999

EMISSION SEQUENCE

Michael Hodder in 1991 suggested this emission sequence based upon studies of coins in various metals that he had studied up to that time:

Group I:
Newman 1-A, Dies 1-A.1 (Brass)
Newman 1-B, Dies 1-A.2 (Brass)
Newman 1-B, Dies 1-A.2 (Brass and
        Pewter)
Newman 1-B, Dies 1-A.2 (Brass and
        Pewter)
Newman 1-C, Dies 1-A.3 (Pewter)
Newman 1-C, Dies 1-A.3 (Silver)
Newman 1-C, Dies 1-A.3 (Pewter)
Newman 2-C, Dies 2-A.3 (Pewter)

Group II:
Newman 3-D, Dies 3-B (Pewter)?
Newman 3-D, Dies 3-B (Silver and
        Pewter)
Newman 4-D, Dies 4-B (Pewter)
Newman 3-D & 5-D,
    Dies 3-B & 4.1-B (Pewter)
Newman 3-D, Dies 3-B (Pewter)

From the foregoing, it seems probable that no special significance attached to brass in the coiners' minds, as we find brass specimens of 1-A.2 (Newman 1-B) in the same and later states as pewter ones. If brass were a metal reserved for patterns, trials, or die set-up pieces, it is unlikely that brass pieces would be run off after striking had started in the intended metal, pewter. It is possible that the rare 1-A.2's in pewter were themselves trials of the dies and press in that metal, however. If these were the case, then two of the three marriages of obverse 1 must be called trials. But, from the conditions of the survivors of 1-A.1 and 1-A.2 (Newman 1-A and 1-B) in both metals, it is certain that they did circulate for some time.

Similarly, since the two silver 1-A.3's (Newman 1-C) are in a later reverse die state than the majority of the pewter strikes from this combination, it seems likely that the silver strikes also were not patterns or trials, but an integral part of the coinage of this combination, whatever their intended currency purpose, if any.

The same close relationship between silver and pewter strikes can be seen in combination 3-B (Newman 3-D), where the two metals appear to have been struck contemporaneously. Pewter 3-B's in a perfect reverse state may exist; if so, they would be the earliest use of this reverse. It should be stressed, however, that no perfect reverse B (Newman's D) has been seen to date. Judging from their reverse states, pewter 4-B's followed the mintage of many pewter and both silver 3-B's, to be followed in turn by whatever number of 4.1-B's were struck in pewter. However, as we now know, an additional quantity of pewter 3-B's followed the probable retirement of 4.1. The sequence for Group II is more complex than earlier thought.

Newman 1-A • Hodder 1-A1 • W-8430 • CURENCY misspelling. Brass •
Obverse: CURENCY misspelling. *Reverse*: Rings as dotted lines. N.HAMPS
right of MASSACHS. *Notes*: Michael Hodder estimated 12 to 15 known. One
has a plain edge. Breen-1085. *Rarity*: URS-5.

Selected auction prices: **John J. Ford Jr. I Sale** (Stack's, 10/2003), Choice EF
$103,500. **Public Auction Sale** (Stack's, 9/2006), F-12 (PCGS) $18,400,
EF-40 (PCGS) $143,750. **Newman Collection Sale** (Heritage, 11/2018),
AU-50 $282,000. **FUN Sale** (Heritage, 1/2015), MS-63 $376,000.

MS-60
—

Newman 1-A • Hodder 1-A1 • Whitman-8432 • CURENCY misspelling.
Pewter • *Obverse*: CURENCY misspelling. *Reverse*: Rings as dotted lines.
N.HAMP'S right of MASSACHS. *Notes*: Plain edge. Discovered in 2014 and
now in a Nevada collection.[1] *Rarity*: URS-1.

Hodder: This was the earliest combination struck; the fact that the final
appearance of this reverse, state A.3 (Newman-C) with dotted rings almost
completely cut into lines, is identical in type (excepting only the reposi-
tioning of N.HAMP'S and MASSACHS) to reverse B (Newman-D),
makes it likely that A.3 predated B despite the lack of die links between the
two. Newman was probably correct in supposing that his reverse A was the
original design and was the first struck, since a progressive change from
dotted to linear rings can be seen on the dies, and the former design was
not utilized on reverse B. Obverse 1 in this marriage is known only in a

perfect state. Its later fate, married to the late state of reverse A (Newman-C), is described below.

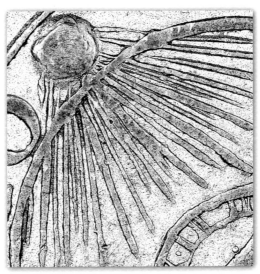

The Roman Numerals on the sun dial were punched into the die as I II III IIII V VI VII VIII XI X IX IIX, my type 1.

Reverse A.1 shows many minute repairs, re-cuttings, and breaks. The last A in AMERICAN has been boldly repunched, as has the W in DELA-WARE. Small die breaks can be seen in YORKE (from K up to the nearest dot), in N.CAROLIN (from A down to the nearest dot), and within the circle under R ISLAND (below IS). In S.CAROLIN the CA are separate; the D in MARYLAND is perfect; and there is no break in the A of VIR-GINIA. If these re-cuttings are not simply the results of poor workman-ship, they may suggest that earlier states might at one time have existed, or that the die-cutter was dissatisfied with his original work and improved it before releasing his dies to the coiners.

Newman 1-B • Hodder 1-A2 • W-8435 • CURENCY misspelling. Pewter
• *Obverse:* Same as preceding. *Reverse:* Dots partly cut into lines. *Notes:* Not known to Newman. Breen-1086. Michael Hodder reported one example that tested as 71.5 percent tin, 26.4 percent lead and the balance other metals; possibly a soft metal trial strike. *Rarity:* URS-2.

Selected auction prices: **FUN Sale** (Heritage, 1/2015), MS-64 $199,750. **ANA Sale** (Stack's Bowers, 8/2018), AU $31,200. **Newman Collection Sale** (Heritage, 11/2018), AU-55 $57,600.

Newman 1-B • Hodder 1-A2 • W-8440 • CURENCY misspelling. Brass • *Obverse:* Same as preceding. *Reverse:* Dots partly cut into lines. *Notes:* Breen-1087. *Rarity:* URS-4.

Hodder: The most obvious feature of reverse A.2 (Newman-B) is found in the rings, which, as is well known, have been partially re-cut into lines. Remnants of the original dotted rings can plainly be seen on many parts of the die. However, there are other, more subtle, differences between A.1 and A.2 (Newman-A and B), among them the additional link-shadowing added to the rings (missing from A.1). Three important features on the die allow us to discover several intermediate states in its life.

Besides the re-cuttings and repairs described on reverse A.1 above, the die was further re-worked; however, some changes made to A.1 can still be seen on A.2. Additional changes include the following. The W of DELAWARE has been re-cut on A.2, eliminating most of the traces of the repunching seen on A.l. Similarly, the D in MARYLAND was also changed, with an I punched over the upright of the D and rotated to follow the curvature of the ring below. This corrected the misshapen appearance that letter had on A.1. In CONNECT,T the second C has been re-engraved; in S.CAROLIN both the A and O have been re-engraved but the underlying letter shapes can still be seen; in MASSACHS the first A and the H have been re-engraved; and in N.YORKE the N has also been re-engraved. Finally, a small break has developed on the A of VIRGINIA and the CA of S.CARO-LIN are joined, features absent on A.1.

In its earliest state, seen only on brass specimens to date, attempts at correcting the small breaks from the K of N.YORKE and the A of N.CAROLIN can be seen. The breaks appear to have been ground down, deepening the fields above those letters. In the case of the latter, the break was fully removed, and I have seen no specimen of A.2 showing a partially repaired break there. In the case of the former, however, there are two distinct states of the repair. At first, the repair was half-hearted and the break can still be made out on the coins. Later, the break was fully ground off the die and no trace of its former presence can be seen. I have found examples struck in brass showing the first stage of repair to N.YORKE. Both pewter specimens show the first stage repair, also. The fully repaired break has been seen only on brass specimens.

In its latest state, which I have noted only on the brass 1-A.2 sold as Garrett:1489, a break or area of die rust has developed within the ring containing PENNSILV. The exact nature of this feature is unknown to me as I have worked from photographs of this specimen only. However, unless the feature is an accident to this particular piece, it represents the latest state of this die. Its shape and direction are quite different from a similar feature seen in the same position on A.3 in combination with obverse 2.

Obverse 1 is always found in perfect condition in this combination. I have seen no signs of minute re-cutting on the obverse of any 1-A.2 I have studied.

Selected auction prices: **Garrett III Sale** (B&R, 10/1980), EF "copper" $11,000. **Roper Sale** (Stack's, 12/1983), EF $8,250. **Norweb II Sale** (3/1988), VF $12,100, EF $15,400. **Americana Sale** (Stack's, 1/2007), AU-55 $207,000. **Los Angeles Sale** (Heritage, 8/2009), MS-63 $299,000. **Newman Collection Sale** (Heritage, 11/2014), MS-62 $440,625. **FUN Sale** (Heritage, 1/2015), AU-55 $182,125. **FUN Sale** (Heritage, 1/2015), AU $88,125.

VG-8	F-12	VF-20	EF-40
$25,000	$35,000	$65,000	$115,000

Newman 1-C • Hodder 1-A3 • W-8445 • CURENCY misspelling. Pewter •
Obverse: Same as preceding. In its late state, often seen, the obverse die has a break over GI in FUGIO; Newman calls this 1.1-C. *Reverse:* The preceding die was heavily lapped and reworked. The rings are now circles composed of thick lines. A comma after AMERICAN is now a period. *Notes:* Ford's finest was "nearly choice brilliant Uncirculated." Edge is often a series of widely spaced diagonal slots or depressions. One is on an overly large planchet. Breen-1089. One with a plain edge was sold in the Pine Tree auction of April 1975. *Rarity:* URS-10.

Hodder: Reverse A.3 represents a radical lapping and revision of A.2, so radical, in fact, as almost to justify calling it an entirely different die. All the diagnostic re-cuttings described above seen on A.1 and A.2 were removed when the die was thoroughly lapped to make A.3. Rather than being a simple re-cutting of the dotted rings into full lines, with some associated re-touchings here and there as Newman described, the die was completely re-worked, the dotted lines mostly ground off and replaced by full lines. In places the underlying dots still remain visible, however. The comma that followed the N of AMERICAN on A.2 became a period when the die was lapped, rather than being re-cut into one. The additional shadowing added to the rings on A.2 disappeared when the die was lapped. Unfortunately, there are no salient features of reverse A.3 in this marriage that allow us to discover a relative chronology for it.

In this combination, however, obverse 1 began to show signs of its age that finally forced its retirement from service. In its earliest state, obverse 1 is found still perfect. Then a thin break develops which connects the upper right serif of G to the upper left serif of I in FUGIO. The die fails further at this point, and the break grows into a pronounced cud covering the tops of G and I. Later still, subsidiary breaks grow from the cud; one following the line of the outer circle and emerging from it under the second N and the space between that letter and the neighboring T of CONTINENTAL, where it forms its own cud which joins the bottom tip of N and the lower serif of T. This branch break continues on through the base of the second T, ending at the A beside it, where another, smaller, cud forms. The other subsidiary break also follows the line of the outer circle, but only for a short distance, emerging above the center of the right side of U in FUGIO. From there it branches upward, engaging the lower right serif of the left stroke of the first N, continuing on to reach the top right of O, and thence to the border beading.

Late obverse state pewter specimens are known showing all stages of the obverse break, from perfect to near collapse. Perfect and early (before the break over GI became a cud) state specimens are somewhat scarcer than later state ones. The commonest Uncirculated specimen is an example of the later states of the obverse. The evidence of the two silver specimens for their die states is controversial because it is unappreciated as yet. The obverses of both Garrett:1491 and Romano:24, the two known, were in the middle stage of development of the break, the cud over GI being prominent but no subsidiary breaks evident. However, on Garrett:1491 the N of CURENCY was weak, apparently from die failure at that position. Romano:24 showed further weakness at that point, with evidence of further die failure which had engaged the neighboring C and reached through the two inner circles to weaken the top of the sun dial and most of the gnomon.

The obverses of both silver specimens had pronounced "bifurcations" at the bottoms of the letters NTIN, features not seen on any of the pewter specimens I examined. These are probably the result of radial metal flow, and their appearance on these two silver specimens only may be a result of their metal. Similarly, no pewter specimen studied showed the die failures at N of CURENCY seen on the two silver ones. It is quite possible that the two silver specimens represent the latest use of obverse 1, following regrinding of the die to remove the subsidiary breaks. This would explain the presence of the cud over GI, which might have been thought too large to fully remove without endangering the whole die. Further supporting the theory that the silver 1-A.3's were the latest use of the dies, is the observation that the shading lines at the inner junctions of the reverse rings are sharp and well outlined on pewter specimens while they are blurred and indistinct on the two silver ones. This observation could also be explained by the differences in metal type, however.

Selected Auction Appearances of Newman 1-C • Hodder 1-A3 • W-8445 • CURENCY Misspelling. Pewter.			
VG–VF	$5,520, Stack's, March 2002	**AU**	$34,500, Heritage, May 2007
	$6,900, B&M, July 2002		$32,200, Heritage, Aug. 2007
	$4,715, Goldberg, Sept. 2002		$34,500, Stack's, Jan. 2008
	$12,650, B&M, Dec. 2003	**MS-60–62**	$25,300, Heritage, Aug. 2001
	$7,188, Scotsman, July 2004		$52,900, B&M, Nov. 2002
	$11,500, Stack's, Sept. 2006		$28,175, Heritage, May 2003
	$14,950, Stack's, Jan. 2007		$34,500, B&M, Sept. 2003
	$14,950, Stack's, April 2007		$48,875, Heritage, Aug. 2004
EF	$8,338, Heritage, July 2002		$92,000, Stack's, Sept. 2005
	$23,000, Heritage, July 2005	**MS-63**	$54,625, Stack's, Oct. 2003
	$29,900, ANR, Oct. 2005		$57,500, Smythe, March 2004
	$29,900, Stack's, March 2007		$63,250, Superior, Aug. 2004
AU	$14,950, Stack's, Jan. 2001		$109,250, Heritage, July 2005
	$19,550, Heritage, July 2002		$92,000, Heritage, Jan. 2007
	$46,000, Stack's, Oct. 2003	**MS-64**	$43,700, Heritage, April 2002
	$28,750, Superior, Aug., 2004		$126,500, B&M, June 2005
	$34,500, B&M, June 2005		$149,500, Heritage, Nov. 2005
	$57,500, B&M, Sept. 2006		$138,000, Heritage, Oct. 2006
	$57,500, Stack's, Jan. 2007		$161,000, Heritage, May 2007
	$40,250, Goldberg Feb. 2007		

G-4	F-12	VF-20	EF-40	AU-50	MS-60	MS-63
$7,750	$12,000	$25,000	$35,000	$50,000	$70,000	$115,000

Newman 1-C • Hodder 1-A3 • W-8450 • CURENCY misspelling. Silver •
Obverse and reverse: Same as preceding. *Notes*: Two known, the Garrett coin and one in the Don Corrado Romano Collection sale (Stack's 1987). Breen-1091. Struck on a cut-down Spanish-American 8 reales. *Rarity*: URS-2.

Selected auction prices: **Garrett III Sale** (B&R, 10/1980), VG $95,000, later in the **John J. Ford Jr. I Sale** (Stack's, 10/2003), $287,500. **John J. Ford Jr. VII Sale** (Stack's, 1/2005), VF $345,000. **FUN Sale** (Heritage, 1/2015), EF-40 $1,527,500.

Newman 2-C • Hodder 2-A3 • W-8455 • CURRENCY. Pewter • *Reverse*: Same as preceding. *Notes*: Ford's finest was a prooflike gem Mint State. Breen-1092. The National Numismatic Collection has a partial trial strike on a small copper planchet, gift of Stack's. *Rarity*: URS-10.

Hodder: Despite efforts at preserving obverse 1, its ultimate failure required a new obverse for the coinage. This die's most salient feature is the corrected spelling of "currency." The 2-A.3 combination is fairly common, being a low Rarity 3 like its predecessor, 1-A.3. To date, specimens are known in pewter only.

Obverse 2 shows no deterioration over its life, even in combination with the latest state of reverse A.3. Since we have seen that the coiners were parsimonious with their dies, allowing obverse 1 to continue in use despite its late, broken state, and even grinding off parts of the break to prolong its usefulness; and re-working reverse A at least three different times; the failure to use the apparently sound obverse 2 in combination with reverse B (. . . Newman's reverse D) later is a perplexing question. Its answer may lie in the distinction between dies 1-A.x and 2-A.3, and 3-B, 4-B, and 4.1-B (Newman combinations 1-A, 1-B, 1-C, 2-C, and 3-D, 4-D, 5-D) . . .

In this combination, reverse A.3 developed a patch of die rust inside the ring below PENNSILV, which progressively grew thicker and longer until it reached almost across the diameter of that ring. Other patches of die rust can also be seen developing on the die, in the rings at MARYLAND at the bottom and N.HAMP'S at the top of the die. The die is known in perfect condition, with faint traces of rust, noticeable traces, and heavy rust. Combination 1-A.3 does not show this rusting, and it is clear that 2-A.3 followed the former in time. However, as A.3 is also known in a perfect state (although this state is rarer than the rusted state), it is possible that some 2-A.3 may have been struck before obverse 1 was finally retired. This is purely speculative on my part, since no other feature of reverse A.3 allows the construction of a relative chronology for it.

	Selected Auction Appearances of Newman 2-C • Hodder 2-A3 • W-8455 • CURRENCY. Pewter.		
VG–VF	$6,325, B&M, Jan. 2001	**AU**	$14,375, Heritage, May 2003
	$6,038, B&M, Jan. 2002		$27,600, Heritage, Sept. 2003
	$18,000, EAHA, April 2005		$29,900, Stack's, Oct. 2003
	$16,100, Heritage, July 2005		$24,150, Heritage, Jan. 2004
	$19,550, Goldberg, Sept. 2005		$29,900, Stack's/ANR, June 2004
	$18,400, Heritage, Apr. 2006		$25,300, B&M, Mar. 2005
	$20,125, Stack's, Oct. 2006		$32,200, Heritage, Jan. 2007
	$17,250, Heritage, Jan. 2007	**MS-60–62**	$24,150, Goldberg, Feb. 2002
	$21,850, Heritage, Aug. 2007		$54,050, Superior, Sept. 2006
	$19,550, Heritage, Nov. 2007	**MS-63**	$33,350, B&M, Nov. 2001
EF	$8,625, Stack's, Mar. 2002		$92,000, Goldberg, Feb. 2005
	$10,350, B&M, Nov. 2002	**MS-64**	$115,000, Superior, May 2005
	$27,600, Goldberg, Sept. 2005		$230,000, Heritage, Aug. 2009
	$25,300, Stack's, Jan. 2006		$223,250, Heritage, Aug. 2012
	$29,900, B&M, Mar. 2006		$199,750, Heritage, Nov. 2014
	$21,850, Stack's, May 2007	**MS-65**	$188,000, Heritage, Jan. 2015
AU	$20,700, Heritage, Feb. 2001	**MS-66**	$51,750, Stack's, Oct. 2003

G-4	F-12	VF-20	EF-40	AU-50	MS-60	MS-63
$8,000	$13,000	$25,000	$35,000	$50,000	$75,000	$115,000

Newman 3-D • Hodder 3-B • W-8460 • CURRENCY, EG FECIT. Pewter. HAMPS left of MASSACHS • *Notes*: This variety is typically seen well struck, as all features were cut deeply into the dies. The reverse die develops tiny cracks within the Rhode Island and New York rings, which expand and connect to form a crack from Georgia clockwise to partly through Delaware and a crack in North Carolina. The engraving on the reverse is much more carefully done than on the preceding die. *Notes*: Breen-1095. *Rarity*: URS-9 or 10.

Detail of Hodder reverse die A, with crude engraving.

Detail of Hodder reverse die B, with more careful engraving.

Hodder: All specimens I have seen to date show varying degrees of the massive reverse break that must have accounted for the ultimate failure of the die. I have seen no examples with a perfect reverse, although these may exist. If they do, they must be extremely rare.

Obverse 3 is the well-known E G FECIT signature die, although exactly who E G may have been is not absolutely certain. Eric Newman's case for Elisha Gallaudet is stronger than that for any other presently known contemporary candidate bearing those initials. Throughout its life, obverse 3 showed no signs of failure; its retirement must have marked the end of the coinage of Continental Currency pieces.

Concerning the sun dial, on this die numerals have been ordered as I II III //// V VI VII XII X IX IIX, omitting number IX and rendering the conventional VIII as IIX. IV was not cut into the sun dial, to create the fiction that it was behind the gnomon.

In this marriage, the earliest of three for this reverse, the reverse developed a linear break through the centers of the rings on the left side of the die (the viewer's right). In the earliest state I have seen, the break extends from within the rings under MASSACHS through the rings under N.JERSEY and PENNSILV. At this stage of its development, the break does not extend into the ring under CONNECT,T. In its latest state, the break nearly encircles the circumference of the die, running from within the ring under GEORGIA, cutting across the base of the ring under N.HAMP,S, and then continuing in the rings around the viewer's right ending under

DELAWARE; on the viewer's left the break can be seen in the rings beneath N,CAROLIN and S,CAROLIN. Faint traces can also be seen in the rings under MARYLAND and VIRGINIA, but only on sharp specimens in the latest state of the die. 3-B in pewter can be found with early and later states of the reverse break. The two silver 3-B's known (plated in the 1914 A.N.S. Exhibition Catalogue, plate 13 and *The Numismatist*, June 1909, p. 177), appear to be in an early stage of the reverse break, as neither shows the break extending through the ring under CONNECT,T. It would appear, then, that the silver 3-B's were struck nearly contemporaneously with the early pewter 3-B's; and that after whatever number of silver pieces were coined, an additional quantity of pewter 3-B's was struck.

Selected Auction Appearances of Newman 3-D • Hodder 3-B • W-8460 • CURRENCY, EG FECIT. Pewter.			
EF	$25,300, Heritage, July 2005	**MS-60–62**	$33,350, Heritage, May 2003
	$37,950, Stack's, Mar. 2006		$74,750, Heritage, Jan. 2007
	$31,050, Goldberg, Sept. 2007		$47,000, Heritage, Apr. 2013
	$12,075, Stack's, Mar. 2010		$21,150, Heritage, Aug. 2016
	$47,000, Stack's, Feb. 2014		$39,950, Heritage, Aug. 2016
	$10,575, Heritage, Aug. 2015		$26,400, Heritage, Jan. 2018
	$18,000, Heritage, Dec. 2017		$33,600, Heritage, Jan. 2018
AU	$12,650, Goldberg, May 2001		$75,000, Stack's Bowers, Mar. 2019
	$17,825, Heritage, Apr. 2002	**MS-63**	$80,500, B&M, July 2005
	$20,988, B&M, Dec. 2003		$143,750, Superior, Feb. 2006
	$25,300, Heritage, July 2004		$88,125, Heritage, Jan. 2015
	$43,700, Heritage, Nov. 2006	**MS-64**	$43,700, Heritage, Apr. 2002
	$63,250, Heritage, Jan. 2007		$189,750, Stack's, Nov. 2007
	$46,000, Heritage, Jan. 2007		$126,500, Heritage, Jan. 2012
	$38,187, Heritage, June 2014	**MS-65**	$28,750, Stack's, June 2004
	$18,800, Stack's Bowers, Nov. 2016		$235,000, Heritage, Apr. 2016
	$44,650, Heritage, Jan. 2017		$180,000, Heritage, Oct. 2019
	$49,200, Heritage, Aug. 2018	**MS-66**	$184,000, Stack's, Oct. 2003
	$45,600, Stack's Bowers, Oct. 2018		$305,500, Heritage, Nov. 2014
	$39,600, Heritage, July 2019	**MS-67**	$444,000, Heritage, June 2018

G-4	F-12	VF-20	EF-40	AU-50	MS-60	MS-63
$8,500	$15,000	$27,500	$40,000	$55,000	$85,000	$130,000

Newman 1-B • Hodder 41-B • W-8465 • CURRENCY, EG FECIT. Brass •
Obverse and reverse: Same as preceding. *Notes*: Listed as Breen-1094 with the notation "unique?" Listed by Eric P. Newman as R-8 on the Sheldon scale (two or three known). Not presently traced. *Rarity*: URS-1 or 2?

Newman 3-D • Hodder 41-B • W-8470 • CURRENCY, EG FECIT. Silver •
Obverse and reverse: Same as preceding. *Notes*: Breen-1096. Struck on a cut-down Spanish-American 8 reales. Newman coin illustrated. *Rarity*: URS-2.

Selected auction prices: **John J. Ford Jr. I Sale** (Stack's, 10/2003), EF $425,500. **Newman Collection Sale** (Heritage, 5/2014), MS-63 $1,410,000. **FUN Sale** (Heritage, 1/2015), MS-62 $1,527,500.

Newman 4-D • Hodder 4-B • W-8475 • CURRENCEY misspelling. Pewter •
Obverse and Reverse: Same as preceding. *Notes*: Michael J. Hodder estimates
four known. One has a plain edge (Ford Collection). The finest is the Newman
MS (illustrated). Breen-1097. Newman coin illustrated. *Rarity*: URS-3.

Hodder: This variety is known only in pewter and is a high Rarity 7, with
four specimens known. I have studied three of these for this essay. Obverse
4 is commonly referred to as an error reverse, from the apparent misspelling of the word currency. It is interesting to note, however, that the same
"misspelling" occurs on the February 17, 1776 paper currency issue, which
has been thought to have been the prototype for the coinage's obverse
design. It is clear from obverse 4's fate that its employers felt the additional
E in CURRENCEY was unwanted. Judging from the rarity of 4-B, the
correction was made fairly early in its working life.

Reverse B in this marriage appears to be in a later state than seen on many specimens married to obverse 3. On the three examples available to me for study, the reverse break already described is in a late state, running from GEORGIA through PENNSILV on the viewer's right and visible under N,CAROLIN and S,CAROLIN on his left. Clearly at least these three 4-B's were struck after the early 3-B's. The break does not extend into the ring below DELAWARE on the three 4-B's I have studied, while it can be seen there on many 3-B's (Norweb:2456 and 2457, Roper 201, for example), showing that 3-B both pre- and post-dated 4-B.

Selected auction prices: **Roper Sale** (Stack's, 12/1983), EF $6,050. **John J. Ford Jr. I Sale** (Stack's, 10/2003), Choice EF $74,750. **Newman Collection Sale** (Heritage, 11/2014), MS-63 $381,875. **FUN Sale** (Heritage, 1/2015), VF-20 $61,687.

Newman 5-D • Hodder 41-D • W-8480 • Corrected to CURRENCY with Ornament. Pewter • *Obverse*: CURRENCEY die with Y added over second E and ornament added over original Y. *Reverse*: Same as preceding. *Notes*: Three verified: Norweb Collection (to the Donald Partrick Collection); VF example, ex Waldo C. Newcomer, later sold by Spink America, June 1997; VF coin discovered in April 1990. Breen-1098. *Rarity*: URS-3.

> **Hodder**: Obverse 4, with the extraneous E in CURRENCEY, was re-cut, the second E being overpunched by a Y, and the final Y turned into a floriate ornament shaped like an X or St. Andrew's cross. Apart from the re-punching

described, the die appears to be unchanged from its earlier incarnation as the CURRENCEY variety. There are no signs of additional wear or other alterations to it.

In this combination, however, reverse B shows itself to be in the later state of the die, with the break clearly traceable through DELAWARE as well as N,CAROLIN and S,CAROLIN, with definite signs of weakening in the ring below MARYLAND. As such, it is later than many 3-B's seen. Obviously, it is later than its predecessor, 4-B. However, it appears contemporaneous with the later states of some 3-B's seen.

Selected auction prices: **Norweb II Sale** (Bowers and Merena Galleries, 3/1988), AU $50,600. **Los Angeles Sale** (Heritage, 8/2009), EF-45 $276,000. **FUN Sale** (Heritage, 1/2015), AU-58 $329,000.

The Continental Army color guard, playing the fife and drum, while marching in winter during the American Revolution.

Part III

Appendices

APPENDIX

A

Signers of Continental Currency

The following individuals were authorized to sign Continental bills. The spelling of some names is uncertain. This is a trial list and may contain errors.[1]

Adcock, William
Alexander, Charles
Alexander, Mark
All, Isaac
Ash, James
Asquith, William

Baird, Samuel
Baker, Christopher
Barclay, Thomas
Barnes, Cornelius
Barney, John (Joshua)
Barrel, Theodore
Barton, Thomas, Jr.
Bayard, John (member of the Continental Congress)
Bedford, Gunning (Emmery), Jr. (member of the Continental Congress, signer of the Constitution)

Billmeyer, J.
Bond, George
Bond, Phineas
Boyd, John
Brannan, Benjamin
Bright, George
Brisson, S. (found only on counterfeit bills)
Brooks (Brook, Brooke), Clement
Brown, G.
Bryson, S.
Buchanan, R.
Budd, G.
Budd, Levi
Bullock, Joseph
Bunner, Andrew
Caither (Cather), Robert
Caldwell, Samuel
Calhoun (Colhoun), James

Campbell, George

Carker, R. (found only on counterfeit bills)

Carleton, Joseph

Carroll, Daniel

Cather, M. (found only on counterfeit bills)

Christ, R.(H.), Jr.

Chrysiler, J.

Cist, Charles

Clarkson, Matthew (member of the Continental Congress)

Claypoole, James

Clymer, Daniel

Coale, Samuel Stringer

Coale, W.

Coats, William

Cockey (Cokey), John

Coit, Joseph

Colladay, William

Collins, Stephen

Colston, W. (found only on counterfeit bills)

Comegys, Cornelius

Conner, G. (found only on counterfeit bills)

Coombe, Thomas

Copperthwait, George (Joseph)

Couden (should be Snowden, per Newman), J. and U.

Courtenay (Courtney), Hercules

Cox, Paul

Craig, William

Cranch, N.

Creery (Creevy), Hans

Crispin, William

Cromwell, Richard

Davis, R. (found only on counterfeit bills)

Dennier, S. (found only on counterfeit bills)

Donellan, Thomas

Donnell (Donald), Nathaniel

Dorsey, Caleb

Dorsey, John (nominated but not known to have signed bills)

Dorsey, Robert

Douglass, George

Douglass, William

Duncan, David

Duncan, G.

Dundas, James

Edison (Eddison), Thomas

Eichelberger, George

Ellis, Joseph H.

Elms, S.

Epplé, Henry

Evans, Joel

Evans, Joseph H.

Evans, Robert

Ewing, James

Eyres, Henry

Eyres, Richard

Farmer, Lewis

Ferrall, Patrick

Foulke, Judah

Fox, Edwin (Edward)

Franklin, James

Fuller, Benjamin

Gaither (Gater), Edward

Gaither, Joseph

Gamble (Gauble), William

Gardner, Joseph (member of the
  Continental Congress)

Garrigues, J.

Garrison, Nicholas

Gibbs, John (found only on
  counterfeit bills)

Gibson, William

Govett, William

Graff, Jacob

Graff, John, Jr.

Gray, George, Jr.

Gray, Isaac

Gray, William

Grier, G.

Griffith, Dennis

Griffiths (Griffith), John

Gutell, R. (found only on counterfeit
  bills)

Hahn, M.

Hammond, William

Hardy, William

Harvey, D. (found only on counterfeit
  bills)

Hazlehurst, Isaac

Hazlehurst, Robert

Hazelwood, John

Helm, John

Herandez, C.

Hewes, Josiah

Hiener, Casper

Hiester, Joseph

Hillegas, Michael

Hillegas, Samuel

Hopkinson, T.

Houston, J.

Howard, John

Howell, Isaac

Hubley, Adam

Hubley, Joseph

Humphreys, Richard

Irwin, Robert

Jackson, William

Jacobs, Benjamin

Johns, Richard

Johnson, Horatio

Johnson, Rinaldo

Johnston, James

Jones, Robert Strettle

Jones, Jno.

Kaighn, John

Kammerer, Henry

Kean, J.

Kelso, John (James)

Keppele, John

Kerr (Ker), John (Joseph)

Kimmell, Michael

King, John (found only on counterfeit
  bills)

Kinsey, Philip

Kuhl, Frederick

Kuhn, J.

Kurtz, Peter

Lardner, John

Laurence (Lawrence), John

Laurence (Lawrence), Thomas

Leacock, John

Leech, Thomas

Leiper, Thomas

Lester, G.L.

Levan, Daniel

Levy, Benjamin

Lewis, C.

Lewis, Ellis

Lewis, Francis, Jr.

Lewis, Mordecai

Limen, W.

Little, James

Loughead James

Lux, Darby

Lux, William

Lyon, Samuel

Maccubin (Mackubin), Zachariah

Mahon, M.

Marshall, William

Masoner, Jacob

Massey, Jacob (Samuel)

Masters, William

McAlester, R.

McCallister (Macallister), A.

McHenry, John

Mease, John

Meredith, Samuel (member of the
    Continental Congress)

Mifflin, George

Milligan, James

Mitchel, C.

Momegan, W.

Morris, Anthony, Jr.

Morris, Luke

Morris, Samuel C.

Morris, Thomas

Muir, F.

Mullen (Mullan), Robert

Nesbit, Alexander

Nesbit (Nesbitt), John Maxwell

Nevill (Nevell), Thomas

Nicholas, Samuel

Nicholson, John

Norris, Aquila

Nourse, Joseph

Ord, John

Paisley, I.

Parker, Joseph

Parr, C.

Patterson, George

Patton, John

Peale, St. George

Pearson, Isaac

Pennell (Pennel), Joseph

Peters, T.

Phyle (Phile), Frederick

Philpot, John

Purviance, John

Ramsey (Ramsay), William

Read (Reed), James

Read (Reed), John

Redman, Joseph

Reintzel, D.

Roberts, Robert A.

Roberts, Robert, Jr.

Ross, James

Rothrock, J.

Round (Rownd), Hampton

Rowan, James

Royson, James

Rush, William

Russell (Rusell), T.

Ryves, E. (nominated but may not
    have signed bills)

Saltar (Salter), John

Salter, William (found only on counterfeit bills)

Schreiner, Jacob

Scott, William

Sellers, John

Sellers, Nathan

Sellers, Samuel

Shaffer (Shaffer, Schaffer), David, Jr.

Shaw, John, Jr.

Sheaf (Sheaff, Sheaffer), William

Shee, John

Shee, Walter

Shoemaker, Charles

Short, J.

Shubart, Michael

Simmons, Luson (Ludson)

Sims, Joseph, Jr.

Smith, Belcher Peartree

Smith, Jonathan Bayard (member of the Continental Congress)

Smith, R. (nominated but not known to have signed bills)

Smith, Thomas

Smyth, John

Snowden, Jedediah

Snowden, Joseph

Spear, William

Sprogell, Ludovic

Stewart (Stuart), D.

Stretch, Peter

Stretch, William

Stringer, Richard

Strong, Matthew

Summers, D. (found only on counterfeit bills)

Swaine, Francis

Sweeney (Sweney), T.

Taylor, John

Thompson, James

Thomson, John

Thorn (Thorne), William

Tilghman, Tench

Tuckniss, Robert

Tybout, Andrew

Wade, F.

Walker, James

Walter, Joseph

Warren, Joseph, Jr.

Warren, Thomas

Watkins, Joseph, Jr.

Watson, J.

Webb, William

Welch, George

Welter, D. (found only on counterfeit bills)

Wetherell (Wetherill), Samuel, Jr.

Wharton, James

Whelen, Israel

Williams, John (member of the Continental Congress)

Wilson, James (member of the Continental Congress, signer of the Declaration of Independence[2])

Wilson, Joseph

Wistar (Wister), Daniel

Wright, John

Young, John, Jr.

Young, G. (found only on counterfeit bills)

Young, Moses

Young, William

APPENDIX
B
The 1783 Treaty of Paris Medal

*T*he Treaty of Paris medal is listed as Betts-614 in *American Colonial History Illustrated by Contemporary Medals*. Dated 1783, it commemorates the peace treaty between the United States and Great Britain signed on September 3, 1783 (the medal mistakenly gives the date as September 4).

The obverse is a cityscape of London and the reverse is a close copy of the Continental dollar reverse but was never used on a coin. The typical weight of the medals is from about 341 grains to 367 grains, as compared to the standard of 255 grains for the Continental dollar.

Following is the description by John Kraljevich of the John W. Adams Collection's medal, sold as lot 23089 for $17,725 by Stack's Bowers Galleries in November 2015:

Rare and Enigmatic 1783 Felicitas Britannia et America Medal

Reverse and Edge Imitating the 1776 Continental Dollar. Betts-614 1783 Felicitas Britannia et America medal. Betts-614. White metal, 38.5 mm. Choice Extremely Fine. 341.9 grains. Decorated edge.

One of the stars of this collection, an extremely rare medal struck to commemorate the end of the American Revolution. The reverse of this medal, an exacting copy of the reverse of the 1776 Continental dollar, suggests that this medal was struck for an American audience. The edge displays a twin-leaf pattern that also imitates that of a Continental dollar, which was in turn borrowed from the edge of a Spanish milled dollar or 8 reales. The surfaces are lively for one of these, retaining hints of silvery luster around design elements on both sides. Elsewhere, the fields have mellowed to pleasing pewter gray, even and appealing. No heavy marks are present, nor any of the seeming attempted punctures seen on so many specimens of this rarity. A light old scratch crosses between TA of FELICITAS to the field above St. Paul's, and a few other trivial scrapes are seen in the upper right obverse. The rims and edges are intact and well-preserved. The planchet is well made, with no visible defects from its initial casting.

One of the most important and notable of all Betts medals, Betts-614 continues to puzzle most students of the series. The quality of its execution, both in terms of die work and minting production, hardly compares to even the crudest British-made medals of the era. Of course, there were poor engravers on both sides of the Atlantic, and America had no monopoly on crudity, but most cheap medals made in England in the era were either better engraved, struck on better planchets, or both. The reverse type would clearly mean more to Americans than to Englishmen in 1783. Even if the Continental Dollar was not widely familiar to Americans (there's no reason to think the coins circulated either far or wide), the paper currency bearing the same design was exceedingly common in the era and was produced in awe-inspiring numbers.

Quite a few Continental dollars appear to have been taken to England as war souvenirs, but these were still considered curiosities long after this medal was struck. (We do not subscribe to the ill-considered new theory that Continental dollars were struck in England as medals, but that deserves more ink than we can spill here.) The edge device of this medal is particularly unusual. Not only did medals rarely have any edge device at all in this era, an edge device that is a near twin to that found Continental dollars makes this medal really, truly unusual. The designer of this medal was not only familiar with Continental dollars, but consciously copied its edge, an edge that was itself a direct copy of that found on Spanish milled dollars of the Pillar type, commonplace in American circulation though by 1783 they had not been struck for over a decade.

This medal would be easier to understand if the reverse die was actually used on Continental dollars, but it was not. It certainly could be a die that was intended to be used in the Continental dollar series, but no coins from this die have ever been recorded. The medal would likewise be easier to understand if the obverse design was different, but all indications are that the skyline depicted is that of London, including the distinctive dome of

St. Paul's Cathedral. While Sir Christopher Wren's architectural masterpiece would have been familiar to most Americans, why would an American engraver depict a London skyline on a medal struck for the American marketplace? The date given on the obverse of the medal has received some comment, including the assertion that the date given—September 4, 1783, rather than September 3, the date the treaty was signed—was the date that the treaty reached London. This appears to be as unlikely as it is unsubstantiated. Newspapers in both London and the United States had been giving updates on the coming close of negotiations for weeks, including false suggestions that the signing was nigh. The actual text of the treaty was not published in London until September 29. Given that the closest port to Paris is Le Havre, 120 miles away, it appears impossible that even a

1783 Treaty of Paris medal.

relay of post riders could have gotten news to London from Paris over-
night. Rather than the date the treaty arrived in London, the date given on
the medal appears to be nothing more than an engraving error.

It is the opinion of this cataloguer that Betts-614 was struck in America for
an American audience. The technical considerations of striking, edge device,
composition, and planchet production fit better in the context of an American minting operation than one in London or Birmingham. The context
does also: events worthy of commemoration with medals usually saw several
different medals struck by competing English shops. The fact that no other
English medals exist to commemorate the Treaty of Paris suggests that
English medalists and toymakers did not foresee demand for souvenirs
marking the treaty. Medals were struck in Germany (Betts-608 and Betts-
610), France (Betts-611 and 612), the Netherlands (Betts-609). None were
struck in England, nor were non medallic commemoratives like textiles,
ceramics, and the like produced by English makers to mark the occasion.
Clearly, the American market was a natural constituency for medals marking
the war's official end. Few designs symbolized the American union better
than Franklin's linked rings concept, and the design was seen on everything
from water pitchers to flags. For the obverse, whose legends cited the friend-
ship of Britain and America, the choice to depict the London skyline was
really a natural one, as London was still the center of the English-speaking
wor[l]d. Though the nascent United States had several cities that were argu-
ably the seat of its civilization, England clearly had but one. The distinctive
dome of St. Paul's and the nearby column of the Monument to the Great
Fire gave an engraver of limited skill an easier task than making the skylines
of New York, Philadelphia, or Boston identifiable to the layman. Had any of
those cities been rendered, numismatists might still be arguing about which
city of low wooden buildings interrupted with the occasional steeple the
engraver had intended. The argument that an English engraver would be
more likely than an American one to depict Britannia sitting and America
standing is specious, as the typical allegorical rendering of Britannia is her
sitting with her shield (as rendered on the George III halfpence, for interest
[. . .]) while the common period rending of America was as a standing native.
The allegory here is both commonplace and lacking in originality.

The primary evidence against an American origin for this medal is the
fact that many of the known specimens have an English provenance. This

may not mean much, as most of those provenance chains begin in England in the mid to late 20th century, a century after Englishmen had been actively collecting many Betts-listed pieces as part of cabinets of English medals. A few have older English provenances. The example sold by Baldwin's in their 2010 Auction 65 was from a cabinet formed before 1852 (along with items like Rosa Americana coins and a Virginia halfpenny). The lovely specimen in the British Museum was donated by Edward Hawkins, a mid 19th century numismatist; it is telling that the BM did not own a specimen decades earlier. Two specimens were identified in American collections before 1875, as cited by Crosby in *Early Coins of America*, one in the collection of William Sumner Appleton, the other owned by Henry Holland. Appleton first published his in 1866. Dr. Charles Clay of Manchester, England owned one, sold in New York in the 1871 auction of his collection, along with dozens of other American colonial pieces. By the time of the 1882 Bushnell sale, the Chapman Brothers reported that "four or five" were known.

There are fewer than 15 of these medals known today, most in rather sorry condition. There was only one in the John Ford collection, sold in our Ford I sale of 2003 along with his Continental dollars. Eric Newman owned one, a low grade piece formerly from Col. E.H.R. Green, also sold with his Continental dollars. Others have graced the cabinets of Lucien LaRiviere, Mrs. Norweb (the same piece brought over $88,000 in the recent Partrick sale), and John Work Garrett. The C.W. Betts piece is in the collection at Yale, the Charles P. Senter example is in the American Numismatic Society, the LaRiviere medal is now at Colonial Williamsburg, and the Boyd duplicate (ex the Bowers and Ruddy Scott sale of 1975) is at Mount Vernon. Along with the example in the British Museum, no less than five examples are impounded, perhaps a third of the entire population. Many, even most, are low grade, indicating that this medal was intended for popular consumption, not for the cabinets of the upper class. An unusual proportion of them include circular divots that appear to be attempted punctures, though none are known holed. This example's superb eye appeal and august provenance make it among the most desirable survivors of this important issue and a highlight of the John W. Adams Collection.

Provenance: From the John W. Adams Collection. Earlier, from Baldwin's sale of December 1984, via John J. Ford Jr.

APPENDIX
C
1776 Continental Dollar Copies

*S*truck copies of Continental dollars from newly made dies were created beginning in the nineteenth century. There were no restrikes from original dies, although copies are often called that.

The 1776 Dickeson copy of the Continental dollar was made using letter punches on both sides, in contrast to the hand engraving of the originals.

The most famous is the so-called Dickeson copy, said to have been made to the order of Montroville W. Dickeson, author of the 1859, 1860, and 1864 editions of the *American Numismatical Manual*. However, I have not found specific information attributing him as the maker, although he is certainly a likely candidate. An 1870 auction catalog by Thomas Birch offering Dickeson's Collection offered these lots under medals:

212 Continental Currency, 1776; copy of Continental seal.

213 Perseverando 1778; do do [ditto, ditto]

213 Confederatio 1778; do do

213 Exitus In Dubio Est 1778; do do[1]

The other three medals used the motto and illustration from various Continental Currency bills in combination with a reverse die telling the date of issue, denomination, and quantity issued. By this time the suite of four pieces was well known to specialists, as other offerings dated back to at least the May 14, 1862,

The Perseverando medal illustrates a motto motif from the May 10, 1775, issue of Continental Currency.

"Catalogue of a Choice Collection of Coins and Medals . . . from the Cabinets of Alfred S. Robinson, Numismatist . . ." sale, conducted by Leonard & Co., Boston:

401 Continental Currency, 1775 [*sic*], bronze.

402 Confederation [*sic*], bronze.

403 Perseverando, bronze.

404 Variety of the same series, bronze.[2]

Nothing has been located specifically attributing these to Dickeson. In this era several different numismatists (including Robinson and Dickeson) commissioned engravers to create copies of earlier coins as well as imaginative new designs and combinations.

The Continental dollar copy is easily enough distinguished by its modern character quite unlike the original, including tiny, irregularly spaced denticles inside the raised border. The 1776 date is compact and distant from the legends on both sides, as compared to originals with the date wider and closer to the legends. The letters are from punches, in contrast to the inconsistent hand-engraved letters on the originals. Probably the mintage was a few hundred at most. These are widely collected by enthusiasts in the So-Called Dollar series.

By 1917 the Continental dollar dies and related dies used to strike medals with Continental Currency motifs or permission to use them then fell into the hands of New York City dealer Thomas L. Elder, who made mulings of various obverses and reverses.[3] These are seldom seen today. Circa 1960 John J. Ford Jr., then in possession of the Continental dollar dies, sold them to Empire Coin Company, which had John Pinches, Ltd., in England, make 7,200 strikings in a white metal alloy.[4] Offered at $12.50 each, three for $29, and ten for $59.75, these proved to be very popular, and all were eventually sold.

The dies then went to Robert Bashlow, a New York City dealer, who commissioned the August C. Frank Company, of Philadelphia, to create new hubs and dies. He advertised copies in various metals: 5,000 in bronze, 2,000 in silver (with a tiny S on the reverse), and 3,000 in goldine (brass).[5] It is highly unlikely that the quantities struck came close to the published figures, even though he advertised "Silver Sold Out!" One was struck over a double eagle. Still later, the dies were used by others. After the Frank shop was finished with them, Bashlow donated the Dickeson dies to the National Numismatic Collection in the Smithsonian Institution, thus assuring buyers that no more would be coined.[6]

APPENDIX
D
Red Book Coverage of the Continental Dollar

The first edition of the *Guide Book of United States Coins* debuted in November 1946. The annual retail-price guide would grow to be one of the most influential books on coin collecting. Known among collectors as the *Red Book* and nicknamed "the Bible of the hobby," it would sell 25 million copies by its 75th edition.

Over the years, the *Red Book* has reflected the ongoing nature of numismatic research and the fluidity of market trends. This is well illustrated using Continental Currency as a case study.

The inaugural *Red Book* included slightly less than a page of text and illustrations covering the Continental Currency pieces, under the category of "Tokens and Pattern Coins" (where they were grouped with the 1776 Massachusetts coppers, Nova Constellatio issues, Immune Columbia and Confederatio "cents," and Brasher doubloons).

"The Continental Dollar is extremely rare," the *Red Book* noted, "and it was supposed to have been engraved by someone whose initials were E.G." Numismatic research at the time justified a definitive statement about its monetary role: "It was the first silver dollar struck for the United States." Historical context was further provided: "It was issued eleven years before the first regularly authorized coin which was the Fugio Cent of 1787, with similar devices and legends."

While *Red Book* author R.S. Yeoman and his team of numismatic researchers (led by Stuart Mosher) strove for documented facts and accuracy, items as mysterious as the Continental Currency made some speculation necessary: "It was possibly struck in Birmingham, England, as were so many other coins of the period." More theorizing was evident in the description of varieties: "These coins were struck in silver, pewter and brass; those in silver probably having done service as a dollar."

In the first edition of the *Red Book*, prices for "Continental Dollars," as they were termed, ranged from $25 in Good to $45 in Fine, with the super-rarities unpriced. Six types were cataloged, with a common obverse and two reverses (CURRENCY and CURENCY) illustrated.

This basic information continued. In the 10th edition, the more readily available pieces were priced at $45 or $50 in Good and $70 or $75 in Fine. The EG FECIT variety in silver was priced at $3,000 in Fine. The CURENCY variety in brass was priced at $125 in Good and $200 in Fine.

The 1947 *Red Book* (published in November 1946) offered
the latest numismatic research on Continental Currency.

The 13th edition (published 1959) was the first to include pricing for Uncirculated pieces.

The 14th edition (published in 1960) was the first to put forth Elisha Gallaudet as the possible engraver of the dies.

The 18th edition of the *Red Book*, published in 1964 with a 1965 cover date, introduced Continental Currency to more Americans than ever before: coins were a bona-fide national hobby craze, and collectors bought 1,200,000 copies of the *Red Book* that year. The book's sales eclipsed even those of Dale Carnegie's *How to Win Friends and Influence People* and John F. Kennedy's *Profiles in Courage*. The text of the "Continental Dollar" section continued to change with ongoing research:

Published during the nation's Bicentennial in 1976, the 30th edition of the *Red Book* recategorized Continental Currency and added more pricing.

The Continental Dollars were probably a pattern issue only and never reached general circulation. It was the first silver dollar size coin ever proposed for the United States. The dies were engraved by someone whose initials were E.G. (possibly Elisha Gallaudet). Some of them have his signature "EG FECIT" on the obverse. The coins were probably struck in Philadelphia.

Varieties are caused by differences in the spelling of the word CURRENCY and the addition of EG FECIT. These coins were struck in silver, pewter and brass, those in silver probably having done service as a dollar.

A typographical star set within the "Colonial" section indicated that facsimiles exist of the listed pieces, explained thus: "Copies of certain early American issues were made to provide facsimiles of rare issues that would otherwise be unobtainable. A star has been placed adjacent to such early American coins or tokens, together with the fabricator's name for which corresponding copies are known." For the Continental Currency pieces, the 18th edition included a star with the name of [Montroville W.] Dickeson, and text further noting that "Copies were struck in various metals for the 1876 Centennial Exposition in Philadelphia."

The 18th edition cataloged seven kinds of Continental Currency, the newest identified variety being the CURRENCEY, Pewter. The book noted that two varieties were known of the brass production with the CURENCY spelling. The exceedingly rare silver EG FECIT, listed a few years before at $3,000 in Fine, was this time left unpriced, as it had been in the book's earliest editions. The more readily available pieces were priced at $100 to $125 in Good, $225 to $275 in Fine, and $575 to $625 in Uncirculated.

By the time of the 25th edition, published in 1971, the market for Continental Currency was more mature, as reflected by more grades being priced (Extremely Fine was added in the 20th edition, published 1966). "Pewter coins in original bright uncirculated condition are worth an additional premium," it was noted. The less rare pewter varieties were priced at $200 to $250 in Good. Uncirculated examples had reached $1,400 to $1,550 in retail value.

The 30th edition of the *Red Book* was published in 1976, the year of the nation's Bicentennial. In this edition the Continental Currency was categorized under "Speculative Issues, Tokens & Patterns"—a group that no longer included the 1776 Massachusetts coppers and Brasher doubloons, which had been moved to "Coinage of the States." It was noted that copies of Continental Currency had been restruck from hubbed dies circa 1960—a warning for collectors. By this time, prices for Good examples of the more readily available pewter pieces were up to $1,000 to $1,200. Fine pieces were priced at $2,500 to $3,500. In Uncirculated, dealers were reporting prices of $10,000 to $12,000. (A new car that year would have cost about $5,000.)

The 40th edition, published in 1986 with a 1987 cover date, included new information that "The link design was suggested by Benjamin Franklin." It continued to share the latest numismatic understanding that "The coins were probably struck in Philadelphia." Information on replica pieces was updated to "Copies were struck in various metals for the 1876 Centennial Exposition in Philadelphia and also restruck from hubbed copy dies circa 1961." The market had softened, with prices in Good listing at $800 to $1,000 for pewter pieces, $1,700 to $1,900 in Fine, and $9,000 to $12,000 in average Uncirculated. The 1980 auction of a silver CURENCY piece in the Garrett Sale was noted, and the value of that piece, one of two known, was listed at $95,000.

By the 45th edition (published 1991), the brass varieties were being priced (at $6,000 in Good, $12,000 in Fine, and $17,000 in Extremely Fine), in addition to the pewter and the Garrett Sale silver piece. The pewter pieces were climbing back upward, priced at $1,200 to $1,400 in Good; $3,000 to $4,000 in Fine; and $13,000 to $15,000 in Uncirculated—again, with a note that original (uncleaned) bright Uncirculated pieces command premiums.

The *Red Book*'s narrative of the early 1990s offered more precision and accuracy than earlier text: they were no longer referred to as *Continental Dollars*, but rather as *Continental Currency* pieces. Their fundamental mystery was emphasized: "The Continental Currency pieces probably had some value at the time they were issued, but the exact nature of their monetary role is still unclear." More research was revealed: "Studies of the coinage show that there may have been two separate emissions made at different mints." And more: "A unique variety is known with a cross after the date. . . . The silver coins probably did service as a dollar, while the brass pieces may have substituted for a penny (although this is considered controversial). Pewter coins most likely had a token value only, if they were used in circulation."

The 50th edition (published 1997) broadened the caveat about counterfeits: "Numerous copies and replicas of these coins have been made over the years. Authentication is recommended for all pieces." The *Red Book* now priced Continental Currency in six grades: Good, Fine, Very Fine, Extremely Fine, About Uncirculated, and Uncirculated. The least expensive pewter example was priced at $1,400 (Good), $3,200 (Fine), $4,500 (VF), $6,500 (EF), $9,500 (AU), and $15,000 (Unc).

The wording in the 56th edition (published 2002) was updated to reflect ongoing research. The engraver of the Continental Currency was now identified as "undoubtedly Elisha Gallaudet" (rather than "possibly"). The nature of the silver pieces was more firmly presented: "The silver coins were intended to circulate as a dollar" (rather than "probably did service as a dollar"). The brass pieces no longer were conjectured as a substitute for a penny, but "may have represented another denomination" (an opinion noted to still be controversial). No narrative mention was made of the variety with a cross after the date, but it was given an unpriced line item in the chart, as "1776 CURRENCY—Ornament after date."

The 59th edition of the *Red Book* (published in 2005, with a 2006 cover date) experienced a dramatic restructuring. Frank J. Colletti describes it in his *Guide Book of the Official Red Book of United States Coins*: "In late March and early April 2005, editor Kenneth Bressett, along with Whitman's new publisher Dennis Tucker, editorial director Diana Plattner, and Q. David Bowers, mapped a redesign of the *Red Book*'s information architecture in a sweeping 12-page plan. All were designed to improve the reader's experience, making the book easier to use and more visually attractive." Describing the rearrangement of the pre-federal issues, which include Continental Currency, Colletti wrote:

> [Before,] all of the front-of-the-book material (from Sommers Islands "Hogge" money to post-Revolution Washington tokens and 1792 patterns) was grouped into 10 separate categories ("The British Colonies in America" to "First United States Mint Issues"). In the 2006 *Red Book*, these coins and tokens were arranged into a single pre-federal section, divided into colonial and post-colonial subsections. Continental currency, Nova Constellatio patterns, Fugio cents, and 1792 proposed coinage were grouped under their own heading of "Contract Issues and Patterns."

Notably, the Continental Currency pieces were categorized as federal issues, rather than "colonial" or "pre-federal," making them more akin to the Philadelphia Mint's 1792 pattern coinages.

The 59th-edition *Red Book* reflected new research and numismatic thought on the nature of the issue's various alloys: "Pewter pieces probably served as a dollar, substituting for paper currency of this design that was never issued. Brass and silver pieces may have been experimental or patterns." Eight different configurations were priced in the 59th edition's charts, with the latest research indicating the types or varieties (and quantities known of certain of them):

1776 CURENCY, Pewter (2 varieties)

1776 CURENCY, Brass (2 varieties)

1776 CURENCY, Silver (2 known)

1776 CURENCY, Pewter

1776 CURENCY, EG FECIT, Pewter

1776 CURENCY, EG FECIT, Silver (2 known)

1776 CURRENCEY, Pewter

1776 CURRENCY, Ornament After Date (2 known)

The market was robust enough for the *Red Book*'s contributors (under the direction of Valuations Editor Jeff Garrett) to give pricing for each variety,

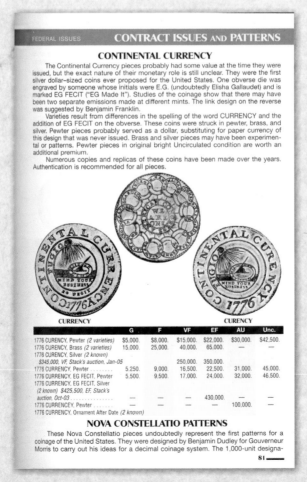

Coverage of Continental Currency in the 59th edition of the *Red Book*.

with the exception of the Ornament After Date. Significant recent auctions were noted for two varieties: the CURENCY, Silver ($345,000, VF, Stack's auction, January 2005), and the CURRENCY, EG FECIT, Silver ($425,000, EF, Stack's auction, October 2003).

In the 65th edition (published 2011), the *Red Book* updated the number of extant pieces of the pewter Ornamented Date variety, from "two known" to three. It noted the July 2009 sale of an Extremely Fine example for $276,000, in a Heritage auction.

By the time the 70th edition of the *Red Book* was published in 2016, the text concerning the pewter pieces was more definitive than in 2005: "Pewter pieces served as a dollar, substituting for paper currency of this design that was never issued." The word *probably* was gone.

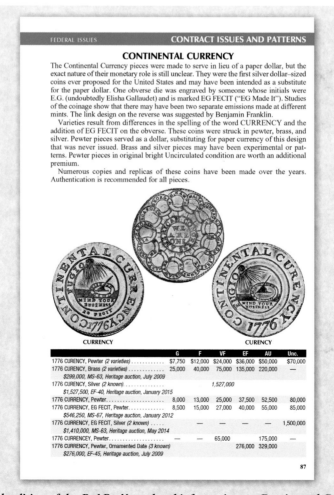

CONTINENTAL CURRENCY

The Continental Currency pieces were made to serve in lieu of a paper dollar, but the exact nature of their monetary role is still unclear. They were the first silver dollar–sized coins ever proposed for the United States and may have been intended as a substitute for the paper dollar. One obverse die was engraved by someone whose initials were E.G. (undoubtedly Elisha Gallaudet) and is marked EG FECIT ("EG Made It"). Studies of the coinage show that there may have been two separate emissions made at different mints. The link design on the reverse was suggested by Benjamin Franklin.

Varieties result from differences in the spelling of the word CURRENCY and the addition of EG FECIT on the obverse. These coins were struck in pewter, brass, and silver. Pewter pieces served as a dollar, substituting for paper currency of this design that was never issued. Brass and silver pieces may have been experimental or patterns. Pewter pieces in original bright Uncirculated condition are worth an additional premium.

Numerous copies and replicas of these coins have been made over the years. Authentication is recommended for all pieces.

CURRENCY   CURRENCY

	G	F	VF	EF	AU	Unc.
1776 CURENCY, Pewter (2 varieties)	$7,750	$12,000	$24,000	$36,000	$50,000	$70,000
1776 CURENCY, Brass (2 varieties)	25,000	40,000	75,000	135,000	220,000	—
$299,000, MS-63, Heritage auction, July 2009						
1776 CURENCY, Silver (2 known)			1,527,000			
$1,527,500, EF-40, Heritage auction, January 2015						
1776 CURRENCY, Pewter	8,000	13,000	25,000	37,500	52,500	80,000
1776 CURRENCY, EG FECIT, Pewter	8,500	15,000	27,000	40,000	55,000	85,000
$546,250, MS-67, Heritage auction, January 2012						
1776 CURRENCY, EG FECIT, Silver (2 known)	—	—	—	—	—	1,500,000
$1,410,000, MS-63, Heritage auction, May 2014						
1776 CURRENCEY, Pewter	—	—	65,000		175,000	—
1776 CURRENCY, Pewter, Ornamented Date (3 known)					276,000	329,000
$276,000, EF-45, Heritage auction, July 2009						

The 70th edition of the *Red Book*'s updated information on Continental Currency.

There were enough sales and auctions of Continental Currency that all eight varieties were priced. Recent auctions were highlighted, including a January 2015 Heritage auction of a CURENCY, Silver, piece (EF-40, $1,527,500) and a May 2014 Heritage auction of a CURRENCY, EG FECIT, Silver (MS-63, $1,410,000).

Numismatists continue to dig into the origins of these arcane pieces of Americana. Will future editions of the *Red Book* firmly state, as some researchers have suggested, that the Continental Currency pieces were actually *medals*, struck overseas, rather than American-made experiments, patterns, and/or substitutes for paper currency? Only time will tell. Numismatics is a living, breathing science, and discoveries are constantly ongoing as historians follow new leads and unearth fresh evidence. The *Red Book*'s editors will continue to update and expand the book's coverage of Continental Currency as the story unfolds.

APPENDIX

E

Diagnostics of Continental Currency Contemporary Counterfeits

From Heritage Auctions' November 7 & 10, 2018, auction catalog of Selections from the Eric P. Newman Collection, Part X.

May 10, 1775, $30 Newman 1.1 Contemporary Counterfeit

Diagnostics: Engraved. Plates cut by Henry Dawkins. This is the first instance of this innovative type of economic warfare.

On the face: In the text, the top of the **R** in **THIRTY** is open. The baselines of **DOLLARS** and **Value** slant down to the right. The period after **1775** is too low compared to that on the genuine bill. Note that it is below the top of the lower curve of the **5** instead of partially above that curve. In the motto, **CIES** of **FACIES** is closer to the outside circle than to the inside circle.

PCGS Very Fine 20. A pleasing example of the scarce Newman 1.1 $30 counterfeit, printed on thick paper.

On the back: The **AR** in **DOLLARS** does not touch at the very top. The ship in the distance in the right vignette does not touch the sun's rays. The last **s** in **Sellers** slants much too far to the right.

Some modest surface soiling is seen, but this is a pleasing example overall. Historically important as the first instance of economic warfare via paper currency.

July 22, 1776, $30 Newman 1.2 Contemporary Counterfeit

Diagnostics: Typeset. Substantially corrected from Newman 1.1.

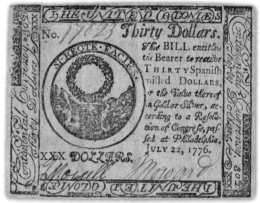

On the face: In the text, the baseline of the word BILL is now level, and the base of the **I** in **THIRTY** is even with the adjacent letters. Three capital letters have been substituted for lowercase letters in **JULY**. The **J** in **JULY** has been moved under the **e** in **passed**. However, the bottom loop of the **C** in **Congress** is still wide open rather than just slightly open, and the left loop of the **P** in **Philadelphia** is still closed.

On the back: In the motto above the left vignette, the top of the **A** in **CONCITATÆ** does not touch the outer circle. The

PCGS Extremely Fine 45. A sharply printed example of this counterfeit, printed on thick paper.

second **s** in **Sellers** has shifted, and its base is now high in relation to the preceding **r**.

Noted as "Pen Cancelled" with the inscription "Counterfeit in No. 132" at the right end of the back. Also noted are "Mounting Remnants and Stain on Back." Faces up very boldly.

May 20, 1777, $8 Newman 1.2 Contemporary Counterfeit

PCGS Choice About New 55. This counterfeit was supposedly a correction of Newman 1.1 except the perpetrators placed the back in the incorrect juxtaposition relative to the face. Printed on thin paper.

Diagnostics: Engraved.

On the face: Same as Newman 1.1, except that the period after **DOLLARS** under the vignette has been added.

On the back: The nature print background has been further muddled to mostly eliminate the crude crosshatching. The back is now in the wrong juxtaposition relative to the face. (The counterfeit bill, when turned horizontally from the face, has the stem of the leaf pointing upward toward the viewer's right rather than downward to the viewer's left on the genuine bill.)

High grade with only some light handling seen.

April 11, 1778, Yorktown Issue $40 Newman 1.1 Contemporary Counterfeit.

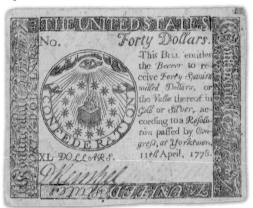

PCGS About New 50. A classic Yorktown issue counterfeit type, printed on thin paper.

Diagnostics: Engraved. This is the second April 11, 1778, $40 described in the Official Broadside.

On the face: In the top border, the right side of the **U** does not reach verticality. Also, the left upright of **A** in **STATES** is thicker than the right upright. In the text, the baseline of **re** in **receive** is far below the baseline of the preceding **to**. The baseline of **th** in **thereof** is much lower than the baseline of **ue** in **Value**. The baseline of **thereof** slants upward to the right. The top of the second **long s** in **passed** is higher than the top of the first **long s**.

On the back: The second **L** in **DOLLARS** does not touch the ornament above it. The nature print background is crudely crosshatched to give it an amateurish mesh-like effect.

Generally a bright example. High grade with light handling.

April 11, 1778, Yorktown Issue $40 Newman 3.1 Contemporary Counterfeit

PCGS Extremely Fine 45. One of several different counterfeit plates observed on the $40 Yorktown notes. Printed on thin paper.

Diagnostics: Typeset. This is the third April 11, 1778, $40 described in the Official Broadside.

On the face: In the text, the top of the **r** in **receive** slants slightly upward to the right. The base of **a** in **ac-cording** is lower than the base of the adjacent **c**. In the motto, the first **N** in **CONFEDERATION** leans to the right. In the vignette, the stars have much larger empty circular centers than on the genuine bill.

On the back: The **R** in **DOLLARS** touches the ornament above it. There are only four pairs of leaves attached to the main stem, rather than five on the genuine bill. The nature print background has been amateurishly engraved with a mesh-like crosshatching and then muddled to obscure it.

Noted as "Pen Cancelled" and indistinct vertically across the right face of the note. Typical wear and face soiling.

September 26, 1778, $40 Newman 1.2 Contemporary Counterfeit

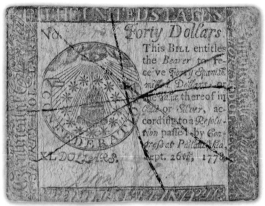 

PCGS Very Fine 20. This deceptive counterfeit is printed on thick paper but also known on thin paper.

Diagnostics: Typeset, very deceptive.

On the face: Same as Newman 1.1 above, except the baselines of **BILL** and **Bearer** are now level and the first **or** has been lowered to its proper position. As on Newman 1.1, in the text, the upright of the **B** in **BILL** is centered under the upright and lower left serif of the **D** in **Dollars** above. The comma after **DOLLARS** is high, and the upright of the **b** in **by** is under the far left of the lower left serif of **R** in **Resolution** above, instead of under the right serif of the word **a**.

On the back: In the nature print, the crude mesh-like crosshatching has been muddled to completely obscure it. In the lower border, the second colon, between ornament numbers eight and nine, is closer to the latter. On the genuine bill, this colon is slightly closer to ornament number eight.

Noted as "Pen Cancelled," with the four crossing cancellation lines spread across the face of the note. A scarce piece.

September 26, 1778, $40 Newman 2.1 Contemporary Counterfeit

PCGS Fine 15. A different counterfeit plate was
used to make this false type, printed on thin paper.

Diagnostics: Engraved. The copper faceplate of this counterfeit is at the
Smithsonian Institution.

On the face: In the text, the base of **m** in **milled** slopes down to the right.
The baseline of the second **to** is higher than the baseline of the adjacent words.
In the motto, the **A** in **CONFEDERATION** is small.

On the back: In the date **1778**, the top of the **1** is higher than the tops of **77**.
Bright for the assigned grade and attractive.

September 26, 1778, $50 Newman 2.3 Contemporary Counterfeit

PCGS Extremely Fine 45. One of the reported
counterfeit plate types for the denomination. The
engraver added typeset commas on the face to
match the genuine note. Printed on thin paper.

Diagnostics: Typeset. This counterfeit may have many variations due to movement or replacement of typeset letters.

On the face: Same as Newman 2.2 except the commas after **Philadelphia** and **26th** have now been corrected by the insertion of typeset commas. To the right of the serial number, the upright of the second **f** in **Fifty** points to the space between the words **the bearer** below it. On the genuine, it points directly to the upper left serif of the **B** in **Bearer**. The baseline of the first **to** is lower than the baseline of **Bearer**. In the motto, the left lower serif of the **P** in **PERENNIS** is present. On the genuine bill, this **P** was broken, resulting in the absence of this serif.

On the back: The top of the **T** in **FIFTY** is higher than the top of the preceding **F**.

A pleasing example with moderate circulation only.

September 26, 1778, $50 Newman 2.3 Contemporary Counterfeit Plate Note

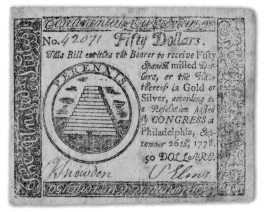

PCGS Very Fine 30. The $50 counterfeits merit their own study due to type movement variations. Printed on thin paper.

Diagnostics: Typeset. This counterfeit may have many variations due to movement or replacement of typeset letters.

On the face: Same as Newman 2.2 except the commas after **Philadelphia** and **26th** have now been corrected by the insertion of typeset commas. To the right of the serial number, the upright of the second **f** in **Fifty** points to the space between the words **the bearer** below it. On the genuine, it points directly to the upper left serif of the **B** in **Bearer**. The baseline of the first **to** is lower than the baseline of **Bearer**. In the motto, the left lower serif of the **P** in

PERENNIS is present. On the genuine bill, this **P** was broken, resulting in the absence of this serif.

On the back: The top of the **T** in **FIFTY** is higher than the top of the preceding **F**.

Noted with "Minor Stains." Wide, apparently full margins from the single-impression plate used. A desirable Newman Plate Note.

September 26, 1778, $60 Newman 1.1 Contemporary Counterfeit

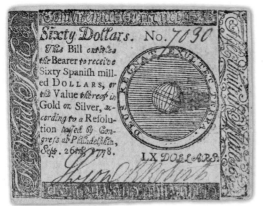

PCGS About New 53. The counterfeits of the $60 type were very deceptive. Printed on thick paper.

Diagnostics: Typeset. Deceptive.

On the face: In the text, the dot over the **i** in **receive** is on the left, instead of slightly to the right, of the dot over the **i** of **milled** below. The base of **x** in **Sixty** is even with, instead of lower than, the base of the subsequent **t**. The upper end of the first **s** in **Con-gress** aims diagonally upward instead of curling downward.

On the back: The bitter end of the top left serif of the **H** in **Hall** points upward.

A very well inked note on both sides. Both false signatures are sharp. A faint vertical fold and some corner handling are seen, but there is not a crease. A choice example.

September 26, 1778, $60 Newman 2.1 Contemporary Counterfeit

PCGS Fine 15. Another deceptive counterfeit type, and rarer than the previous. Printed on thin paper.

Diagnostics: Typeset. Deceptive.

On the face: In the top border, there are no curved brackets surrounding the **n** in **Currency**. In the text, the top left serif of the **v** in **receive** curls downward. The base of the **r** in the first **or** is lower than the preceding **o**. The base of the first **c** in **ac-cording** is low, and the second **c** is small. The top of the comma after **Philadelphia** is above the center of the preceding **a**.

On the back: The tops of the **A** and **R** of **DOLLARS** nearly touch. The top left serif of the **P** in **Printed** touches the center of its upright.

This is a problem-free note with only honest circulation.

Genuine September 26, 1778, $60 Penned "Counterfeit"

PCGS Very Fine 35.

This is an unusual "counterfeit" because it is falsely condemned and fully genuine. The deceptive counterfeits (Newman 1.1 and Newman 2.1) of this type may have caused the confusion. Pen-canceled as "Counterfit [*sic*] In No. 3 of 10" on the face. Printed on thick paper. Noted with "Small Edge Splits." A very intriguing Continental note.

January 14, 1779, $80 Newman 2.2 Contemporary Counterfeit

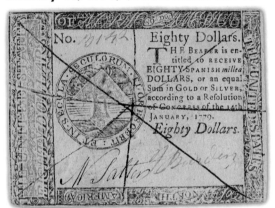

PCGS Extremely Fine 45. A deceptively made counterfeit. Printed on thin paper with the UNITED/STATES watermark. The end of this watermark touches the right side of the note. On this variety, the dot above the "i" in "Printed" has been omitted (as on the genuine note).

Diagnostics: Typeset, very deceptive. This counterfeit may have many variations due to movement or replacement of typeset letters.

On the face: To the right of the serial number, the upright of the **t** in **Eighty** is in line with the right of the **E** in **THE** below. On the genuine bill, the upright of the **t** is over the center of the **E**. In the text, the lower right serif of the **R** in **Resolution** ends over the center of the **f** below it, instead of much to its right. In the motto, the space between **EC** of **SECULOREM** is abnormally wide. The two-color print registration problem has been corrected.

On the back: The dot above the **i** in **Printed** has been removed.

Noted as "Pen Cancelled" with four crossed lines across the face. The color is sharp.

APPENDIX
F

State-issued 1780 "Guaranteed by the United States" Notes

**The earliest federally backed, state-issued paper currency
and a forebear to the United States federal currency system**

*From Stack's October 4, 2006, auction catalog
of the John J. Ford Jr. Collection, Part XV.*

The "Guaranteed by the United States notes," authorized by a single resolution of the Continental Congress in 1780, are a very collectible and important early American paper currency series. These notes, issued by eight of the original 13 states (the original colonies), constitute a subseries of colonial American paper currency that is both an integral adjunct to the Continental Currency series (ending with the January 14, 1779, resolution notes) and the earliest form of a federally backed, state-issued paper currency and interest-bearing note system. A complete major typeset of guaranteed notes includes 64 types: eight denominations from each of the eight states that emitted notes.

The enactment by the Continental Congress of March 18, 1780, authorized the states themselves to embark on a course of Continental Currency redemption, revaluation, and an attempt to stabilize the money supply as necessary. Parts of that enactment read as follows:

> "These United States having been v into this just and necessary war at the time when no regular civil governments were established of sufficient energy to enforce the collection of taxes or provide funds for the redemption of such bills of credit as their necessities obliged them to issue; and

before the powers of Europe were sufficiently convinced of the justice of their cause or of the probable event of the controversy to afford them aid or credit, in consequence of which their bills increasing in quantity beyond the sum necessary for the purpose of a circulating medium and wanting at the same time specific funds to rest on for their redemption they have seen them daily sink in value notwithstanding every effort that has been made to support the same: insomuch that they are now passed by common consent in most parts of these United States at least thirty-nine fortieths below their nominal value and still remain in a state of depreciation whereby the community suffers great injustice, the public finances are deranged and the necessary dispositions for the defense of the country are much impeded and perplexed; and whereas, to effectually remedy these evils for which purpose the United States are now become competent, their independence being well assured, their civil governments established and vigorous, and the spirit of their citizens ardent for exertion, it is necessary speedily to reduce the quantity of the paper medium in circulation, and to establish and appropriate such funds that shall ensure the punctual redemption of the bills; therefore . . .”

Further:

“That the said new bills issue on the funds of the individual states for that purpose established, and be signed by persons appointed by them, and that the faith of the United States be also pledged for the payment of the said bills in case any state on whose funds they shall be emitted should by the events of war be rendered incapable to redeem them: which undertaking of the United States and that of drawing bills of exchange for payment of interest as aforesaid shall be endorsed on the bills to be emitted and signed by a commissioner to be appointed by congress for that purpose.”

This enabling act created the system of state-issued notes guaranteed by the Continental Congress and can be seen as a first, early step toward a federal currency. By this act, the Congress encouraged the individual states to issue legal tender paper currency by guaranteeing and backing its face and interest values by the revenues of the national government. States would cry up outstanding Continental Congress notes of earlier emissions still in circulation within their borders, and for every $40 of the old Continental notes withdrawn from circulation, the Congress would guarantee the value of $1 of the new state issue. States were permitted to use three-fifths of the value authorized for their own circulation needs. The other two-fifths was for the use of the confederation government but helped cover the credit-worthiness of the other states. The notes bore interest at 5 percent per annum, the interest being guaranteed by bills of exchange bought by the Congress on the European market. The cost was ultimately to be borne by the states out of credit accruing to their accounts. To make things easier for the states, but also to give the Congress accounting control over the value of notes, each state was entitled to use the Congress's printers, Hall & Sellers of Philadelphia. They printed the guaranteed notes for each state with a uniform style.

The entire issue was expected to be retired within six years. Since the notes were to be made legal tender by state resolutions and were guaranteed by the Continental Congress, it was hoped the system would create a paper currency with dual backing, a hybrid state/national currency with the benefits of both. Unfortunately, by reducing at one stroke the value of all older Continental notes to 2.5 cents on the dollar, the savings and inventories of those holding the older notes, who had been enticed by patriotism or persuaded by promises to accept them, were wiped out. The system, well-meaning as it was, also led to a general market repudiation of Continental Currency and the ensuing resistance to both a national currency and a national bank that characterized the economic debates of the 1820s and 1830s, culminating in the Jacksonian Bank of the United States fiasco.

The notes for each state were printed in Philadelphia at Hall & Sellers by Congress's order and sent to their respective Continental Loan Offices. The amount sent roughly corresponded to the amount allocated to each state by earlier acts governing the amount of old Continental notes each state was obliged by law to accept. On receipt, the notes were signed on the face by the officials appointed by the state and countersigned on the back by the commissioner appointed by Congress, to the amount authorized for remittance by the state (which was not always the same as the amount authorized for issuance). The signed notes were then locked in the commissioner's office. Holders of older Continental Currency issues brought their currency into the Continental Loan Office and exchanged it at the $40 old to $1 new ratio. Once the loan officer satisfied himself that the old notes presented were genuine, he accepted them in exchange and handed over new, guaranteed bills to the bearer.

Each of the notes issued by the states and guaranteed by the Continental Congress was denominated in Spanish milled dollars (i.e., 8-reales coins, the famous "pieces of eight"). As legal tender, the bearer of the note was promised its full value payable to him or her at any time before December 31, 1786. Virginia's notes bear a handwritten issue date on their faces, above the interest box, and are the only ones to do so (this practice ceased at the end of 1781). To keep the notes in circulation and encourage their widespread acceptance, each paid interest on the face value at the rate of 5 percent annually. As a further inducement to public acceptance of the guaranteed issues, interest was payable monthly as well as annually from the issue date (or other legally stipulated date) and each note was printed with a handy interest table on its face showing exactly how much accrued per month and per year. Each issuing state bound itself to the bearer to pay on redemption the face value plus the accrued interest. Revenues for redemption were expected to be made up from state treasuries, but in lieu of sufficient resources the note was guaranteed by the Continental Congress.

On redemption of interest the note might be surcharged accordingly, as did Massachusetts (with the statement "INTEREST PAID ONE YEAR" stamped in red on its face), New Jersey and Pennsylvania (with the statement "INT. PD. 1 Yr."), and Rhode Island (with the statement "Int. pd. one Yr."). On redemption of face value, the note might be hole cancelled (a parcel of May 5, 1780, Massachusetts guaranteed notes all gang cancelled was described in the July 1939 issue of *The Numismatist*, for example).

The great majority of types (64, to be exact) on this series were not counterfeited. Counterfeiting was a problem for Massachusetts, which saw the higher denominations ($7, $8, and particularly the $20) copied. New Jersey's $5 note was counterfeited and so were Maryland's and New York's $20 notes. However, New Hampshire's, Pennsylvania's, Rhode Island's and Virginia's issues were not copied to our knowledge. The system worked only if the states retained confidence in the Congress's guarantee to find the funds to back the notes and the interest payable on them, and their own ability to pay out for notes when presented for redemption. The delay in sending notes to Connecticut caused that state to refuse to issue them, as by the time they had arrived each had already accrued six months or more interest payable on initial emission. New Jersey's own troubled finances led that state only to issue part of the amount it authorized and then to end the notes' legal tender status as of May 1, 1782, and to progressively devalue them despite the national guarantee. New York's inability to guarantee legal tender status to all $487,500 of its issue of June 15,1780, meant only a small fraction ($70,625) was backed by the national guarantee, while the majority ($416,875) had to be emitted as a normal state issue, although it did pay 5 percent interest to those willing to take a chance on it.

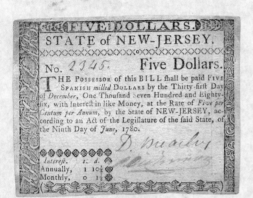

This genuine New Jersey $5 bill, guaranteed by the United States, was one of 12,000 printed as part of the June 9, 1780, issue.

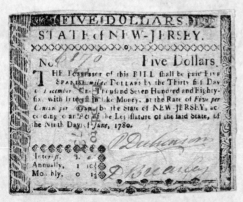

A contemporary counterfeit version of the New Jersey $5 note above can be distinguished by a few diagnostics: the whiteness and texture of the paper; the N in AB-STINE in the motto SUSTINE VEI ABSTINE, located on the back of the note; and the ornaments on the top of the bill face, which are divided 15 left, 13 right of the bullet on the genuine bill and 14 on each side on the counterfeit.

Pennsylvania authorized over a million and a quarter dollars' worth of guaranteed notes on June 1, 1780, but actually issued far less than that amount and kept what it did authorize valid until the summer of 1792. Only part of what Rhode Island authorized was released with a signed guarantee on the back, making the others technically state notes and not state/national hybrid notes (these unsigned notes were ordered exchanged for the succeeding Rhode Island issue of May 1786). A large portion of Virginia's issue of May 1, 1780, was not issued, either.

The states of the Deep South—Georgia, North Carolina, and South Carolina—did not participate in the guaranteed note system. Delaware, which is a southern state even if it doesn't think so, also did not participate. Virginia and Maryland, which have never decided whether they are southern or northern states, did take part in the confederal system, however. Since the system was based upon redemption of old Continental Currency notes, and since the Deep South did not see much of that money due to local self-sufficiency and British occupation of these aboard, it is not difficult to understand why it did not reach those members of the confederated states. Delaware's absence is not easily explainable.

The congressionally guaranteed notes of 1780 are denominated $1, $2, $3, $4, $5, $7, $8, and $20. They all have a common design format and style. The faces bear the name of the issuing state, the note's serial number and denomination, and a statement of the exchange value of the note, its interest rate and term, and space for signatures by state officials (always two for Pennsylvania and Virginia). The statement is worded identically on each state's issue save for the last two lines, which give the issuing state's name and the date of the act authorizing

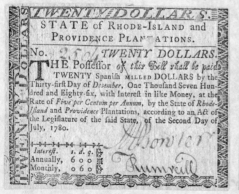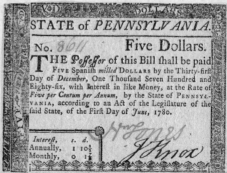

This Pennsylvania $5 note (left) and Rhode Island $20 note are two examples of state-issued paper currency guaranteed by the United States, which were sold at auction as part of the John J. Ford Collection, Part XV, on Oct. 4, 2006.

its issue. The lower left corner of the note bore an easy-to-use interest table showing exactly how much interest it would pay both monthly and annually.

The face color is black. The backs of the notes are a combination of border cuts and emblems taken from the January 14, 1779, issue of the Congress' own notes and engraving cuts by Philadelphia engraver Henry Dawkins. The top and bottom border cuts read 'UNITED STATES' in two different fonts. Above the bottom cut is the statement of guarantee by the Continental Congress and the date of the authorizing resolution. There is space at the base for a single signature on behalf of the Congress. The back colors are red and black singly and in combination. The notes were printed on locally made paper watermarked 'UNITED STATES' (used by Maryland, Massachusetts, and New Jersey issues) or 'CONFEDERATION' (used by the New Hampshire, New York, Pennsylvania, Rhode Island, and Virginia issues).

Commentaries on Individual States That Did Not Issue Notes Based on the "Guaranteed by the United States" System

Connecticut. The issue of June 1780 was intended to be supplied by the notes guaranteed by the Continental Congress that were printed late that month in Philadelphia by Hall & Sellers, the Continental Congress's printers. However, the notes were not sent to the treasurer of Connecticut until the early months of 1781. By then, the notes had already accrued interest that the state would have to pay immediately on emission. Accordingly, Connecticut issued its own state notes of the June 1, 1780, emission, and when the Congress's notes arrived they were held in the treasury and later returned to the (now) United States Treasury, which burned them in 1790 and 1795.

Delaware. Did not request or receive notes guaranteed by the Continental Congress.

Georgia. Did not request or receive notes guaranteed by the Continental Congress.

North Carolina. Did not request or receive notes guaranteed by the Continental Congress.

South Carolina. Did not request or receive notes guaranteed by the Continental Congress.

APPENDIX
G

The Security Printing Genius of Benjamin Franklin

Information from the Stack's Bowers Galleries' August 17, 2011, Chicago ANA Auction catalog, pages 73, 81, and 85–87.

Benjamin Franklin's impact upon American currency was forged from his early life when he was apprenticed to a printer. Throughout his legendary, long, and illustrious life, he always considered himself a master printer and applied much of that acumen and precision in his day-to-day life. Franklin's contributions and ingenuity in security printing and paper currency from 1739 to 1781 were paramount in the evolution of money in colonial America and later the newly formed United States of America.

Franklin began printing currency notes for Pennsylvania, New Jersey, and Delaware in the 1730s. Counterfeiting often plagued many issues and Franklin invented Nature Print backs for currency notes to thwart imitations. Those three colonies used the Nature Print backs for decades, across several issues. His sole "B. Franklin" imprint is extremely rare.

Franklin's influence upon American currency was considerable, with his Fugio designs placed upon fractional Continental Dollar notes denominated from $1/6 to $2/3. The February 17, 1776, bills were the only fractional notes issues in the Continental Congress series. The motifs were created from Franklin's early Poor Richard's almanacs. His motto MIND YOUR BUSINESS on the face of the notes is iconic with present-day numismatists.

His impact on the first 1775 Continental Currency notes is also of immense importance in the emergence of the United States. He designed two patriotic motifs and obtained special marbled paper, impossible to counterfeit, for the first $20 notes.

Franklin used this marbling again on the 1781 American loan certificate, which he printed and signed, for 1,000,000 livres from the French treasury. He obtained the specially woven and marbled paper for the certificate from James Whatman in England. Each sheet of paper was marbled separately down the center of the sheets so that, when cut by hand in a wavy fashion, the halves would form an indented pair that could be rejoined at time of repayment. The process proved to be both challenging and time consuming, leading to a lengthy delay in the delivery of the paper to Franklin, but the addition of the marbling was an integral part of the document.

The security and authenticity of these certificates was a major concern, just as it was when Franklin invented the Nature Print method used to deter the counterfeiting of currency. The multicolor marbled design, impossible to duplicate, served as an absolute deterrent to the counterfeiting of the loan certificates.

Benjamin Franklin at his printing press in Philadelphia.

The 1781 loan certificate was created shortly after the Continental Army's victory at Saratoga and the formation of an alliance between the young United States and France. Franklin was serving as minister plenipotentiary to France at the time, securing financial and military assistance for the Revolutionary War.

In total, France provided 18,000,000 livres across 21 loans to the United States. From the moment he personally negotiated the loan with the French royal government to the instant he took his quill pen in hand to sign the certificate, this was Franklin's endeavor. There is most certainly no other person ever to negotiate a crucial loan with a foreign country and then proceed to print the official document. This certificate was designed and printed with craftsmanship and ingenuity unsurpassed by his contemporaries.

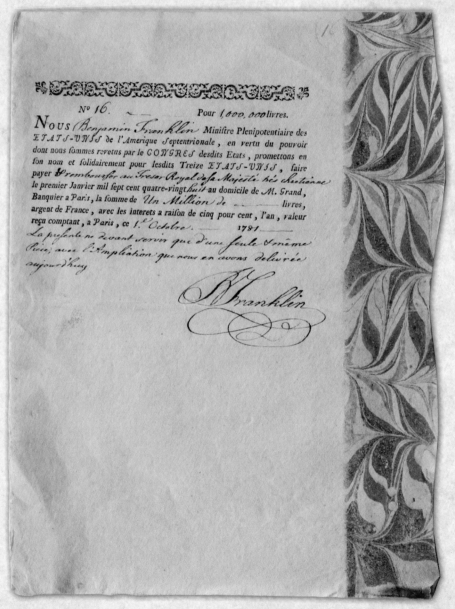

The 1781 U.S. loan certificate, created and signed by Benjamin Franklin, features a marbled border and scalloped edge. It sold for $218,500 at the August 17, 2011, Chicago ANA Auction.

Notes

Certain quotations have been lightly edited and misspellings corrected (the alternative would have been to burden the reader with a long stream of *sic* notations). Ship names and book titles in early notices have been set in italic type in the present text. The use of the "long *s*" (an archaic English letter that looks like a lowercase *f*) in early notices has been changed to the standard *s* for easy readability.

Chapter 1

1. The Georgia contingent made its first appearance when Congress reconvened on September 5, 1775, and were seated on the thirteenth. After this time all colonies were represented.
2. Hunt's *Merchants' Magazine and Commercial Review*, 1850, p. 804.
3. Jared Sparks, *Life of George Washington*, p. 224.
4. *American Archives*, 5th series, 3rd volume.
5. Henry Phillips Jr. *Historical Sketches of American Paper Currency*, 1866, p. 44. In retrospection some such as Benjamin Franklin and Thomas Jefferson placed the time as in the summer.
6. *Ibid*, p. 61.
7. *Ibid*, p. 75 *passim*.
8. *Ibid*, p. 85.
9. Samuel Breck, *Historical Sketch of Continental Paper Money*, 1863, p. 11.
10. Edwin Hall, *Ancient Historical Records of Norwalk, Conn*. Norwalk, CT: James Mallory & Co., 1847, p. 137.
11. *Pennsylvania Gazette*, July 7, 1779.
12. Benson J. Lossing, *Pictorial Field-Book of the American Revolution*, 1855, p. 319. It cost $74 in Continental Currency to buy $1 value in silver or gold coins.
13. W. Winterbotham. *An Historical, Geographical, and Philosophical View of the American United States and of the European Settlements in America and the West-Indies. . . .* Vol. III, Second Edition. London, 1799, p. P. 15.
14. This was in the second edition. The first edition had punctuation that readers said was erratic and often wrong.
15. The federal government only had a minor interest in each. Both banks were widely criticized by the shareholders and officers of state-chartered banks, who stated that the competition was unfair.

Chapter 2

1. No published study of these varieties has been seen.
2. Willcox & Co. was founded in 1729. The company furnished paper for printing certain colonial bills as well as Continental Currency notes and later for notes of state-chartered banks.
3. The process is detailed by Eric P. Newman in "Nature Printing on Colonial and Continental Currency," *The Numismatist*, February 1964, and subsequent issues.
4. The earliest known is a 1739 20-shilling note of Pennsylvania.

Chapter 3

1. Henry Phillips Jr. *Historical Sketches of American Paper Currency*, 1866, p. 30. Over a period of time additional signers were appointed.

2. Information about leaves is adapted from Eric P. Newman, *The Early Paper Money of America*.
3. The features are not easily distinguished.
4. The features are not easily distinguished.
5. Henry Phillips Jr. *Historical Sketches of American Paper Currency*, 1866, pp. 98, 99.
6. A historical marker was erected on the site and dedicated on December 14, 1949.
7. Newman: The genuine signature on the bills is "Jas Wilson," with a small s in the first name high above the preceding letter. An amanuensis substituting for James Wilson also signed "Jas Wilson" with many differences, particularly the lack of a long sweep on the right side of W. The signature of *Joseph* Wilson is always written as "J. Wilson" and thus readily distinguishable from the signature of James Wilson.
8. *Ibid*, pp. 112, 116. In a letter of this era General Washington wrote that "a wagon load of money will scarcely purchase a wagon load of provisions."
9. Newman: The genuine signature on the bills is "Jas Wilson" with a small s in the first name, high above the preceding letter. An amanuensis substituting for James Wilson also signed "Jas Wilson" with many differences, particularly the lack of a long sweep on the right side of W. The signature of *Joseph* Wilson is always written as "J. Wilson" and thus readily distinguishable from the signature of James Wilson.

10. Karl Rhodes, "The Counterfeiting Weapon," Federal Reserve Bank of Richmond *Region Focus*, retrieved from Wikipedia.
11. This paragraph is from chapter 17 in Christopher R. McDowell's book, *Abell Buell and the History of the Connecticut and Fugio Coinages*.
12. Citations under this heading were adapted from Eric P. Newman, "The Successful Counterfeiting of British Paper Money During the American Revolution," *The Numismatist*, 1958. This article contains many more accounts of counterfeiting.

Chapter 4
1. These two issues had been discredited in 1778 and therefore sold at an extremely deep discount to speculators.

Chapter 5
1. John Kleeberg, "The Continental Dollar; British Medals or American Coins?" *Journal of Early American Numismatics*, 2018. In contrast, *Walter Breen's Complete Encyclopedia of U.S. and Colonial Coins*, 1988, p. 110, nondestructive analyses performed on several Continental Currency pieces in 1963–1964; stating that the typical coin is 95 percent tin and 5 percent natural alloys, not including lead; this can be discarded.
2. *Ibid*.
3. Quoted in the *American Journal of Numismatics*, October 1891, p. 45.
4. Joel J. Orosz, *The Eagle That Is Forgotten: Pierre Eugène Du Simitière, Founding Father of American Numismatics*.

5. Revere family papers preserved by the Massachusetts Historical Society.

6. Eagleton, Catherine. *Collecting America: Sophia Banks and the 'Continental Dollar' of 1776*. London: *Numismatic Chronicle*, 2014.

Chapter 6

1. Roach, Steve, "Unlisted pewter variety of 1776 Continental dollar discovered by Heritage Auctions' Brian Koller," *Coin World*, December 12, 2014.

Appendix A

1. This listing was compiled from various sources, starting with Henry Phillips Jr., *Historical Sketches of American Paper Currency*, 1866, continuing to the most important: Eric P. Newman, *The Early Paper Money of America*, 1997. The latter includes the research of Joseph R. Lasser published in *The Numismatist*, May 1975. Joe Lasser was a fine friend and frequent correspondent of mine; he donated his extensive collection to Colonial Williamsburg, presently under the curatorship of Erik Goldstein. Over the years there have been misreadings of many signatures, giving rise to parenthetical alternates. I have corrected many, but others remain to be done.

2. Newman: The genuine signature on the bills is "Jas Wilson" with a small s in the first name high above the preceding letter. An amanuensis substituting for James Wilson also signed "Jas Wilson" with many differences, particularly the lack of a long sweep on the right side of W. The signature of *Joseph* Wilson is always written as "J. Wilson" and thus is readily distinguishable from the signature of James Wilson.

Appendix B

1. Citation provided by William Hyder.

2. Citation provided by Julia H. Purdy.

3. Further described by Thomas K. DeLorey in "Thomas L. Elder, A Catalogue of his Tokens," *The Numismatist*, June and July 1980.

4. These can be identified by a small die scratch under the C of CONTINENTAL.

5. I knew Bashlow well, as he was a customer for many years. Hyperbole and exaggeration came naturally to him. See *The Numismatic Scrapbook Magazine*, August 1962, for a typical advertisement.

6. Sources include Robert Bashlow as well as "Distinguishing Dickenson's Dollars" on the Internet site of DM Rare Coins (adapted from an article, "The Continental Dollar Restrikes," by Jeff Shevlin, February 2006 [per correspondence from him on January 30, 2019]).

Bibliography

1. At the Numismatic Literary Guild Symposium held with the American Numismatic Association convention in August 1977, Lasser spoke on "Signers of the May 10, 1775, Continental Currency Issues."

Selected Bibliography

American Journal of Numismatics. Various issues. New York, NY, and Boston, MA: 1866–1912.

Asylum, The. Various issues. Numismatic Bibliomania Society, 1980–1998.

Atkins, James. *Coins and Tokens of the Possessions and Colonies of the British Empire,* London, England: Bernard Quaritch, 1889.

Baker, W.S. *American Engravers and Their Works.* Philadelphia, PA: Gebbie & Barrie Publishers, 1875.

Betts, C. Wyllys. *American Colonial History Illustrated by Contemporary Medals.* New York, NY: Scott Stamp and Coin Co., Ltd., 1894.

Bowers, Q. David. *The History of United States Coinage as Illustrated by the Garrett Collection.* Published for The Johns Hopkins University, Baltimore. First printing, Los Angeles, CA: Bowers and Ruddy Galleries, Inc., 1979; later printings, Wolfeboro, NH: Bowers and Merena Galleries, Inc.

——. *The American Numismatic Association Centennial History.* Wolfeboro, NH: Bowers and Merena Galleries, Inc. on behalf of the American Numismatic Association, 1991. Two volumes.

——. *American Numismatics Before the Civil War.* Wolfeboro, NH: Bowers and Merena Galleries, Inc., 1998.

——. *The Whitman Encyclopedia of Colonial and Early American Coins.* Atlanta, GA: Whitman Publishing LLC, 2009; second edition, Pelham, AL, 2020.

Breck, Samuel. *Historical Sketch of Continental Paper Money.* Philadelphia, PA: Printed by John C. Clark, reprinted by A.C. Kline, 1863.

Breen, Walter H. *Walter Breen's Complete Encyclopedia of United States and Colonial Coins.* New York, NY: Doubleday & Co., 1988.

Bronson, Henry, M.D. *A Historical Account of the Connecticut Currency, Continental Money, and the Finances of the Revolution.* New Haven, CT: Thomas J. Stafford, Printer, 1865.

Chalmers, Robert. *A History of Currency in the British Colonies.* Colchester, England: John Drury, 1972. Reprint of 1893 edition.

Coin Collector's Journal, The. Various issues. New York City, NY: J.W. Scott & Co., 1870s–1880s.

Coin World. Various issues. Sidney, OH: Amos Press, *et al.,* 1960 to date.

Colonial Coin Collectors Club Newsletter, a.k.a. *C4 Newsletter.* Various issues. The Colonial Coin Collectors Club, 1993 to date.

Colonial Newsletter, The. Various issues. New York, NY: American Numismatic Society, 1960 to date.

Continental Congress, papers and journals, various sources.

Crosby, Sylvester S. *The Early Coins of America*. Boston, MA: Published by the author, 1875.

Dickeson, Montroville W. *American Numismatical Manual*. Philadelphia, PA: J.B. Lippincott & Co., 1859. Also second edition (1860) and third edition (1865), retitled *American Numismatic Manual*.

Doty, Richard G. *America's Money, America's Story*. Iola, WI: Krause Publications, 1998; second edition, Atlanta, GA: Whitman Publishing, 2008.

E-sylum. Various issues. Numismatic Bibliomania Society, 1998 to date.

Eagleton, Catherine. *Collecting America: Sophia Banks and the 'Continental Dollar' of 1776*. London, England: *Numismatic Chronicle*, 2014.

Eckberg, Bill. "Shady Stories for U.S. Coins." *Coin World*, September 24, 2015.

Ellet, E.F., Mrs. *Domestic History of the American Revolution*. New York, NY: Baker and Scribner, 1850.

Felt, Joseph Barlow. *An Historical Account of Massachusetts Currency*. Boston, MA: Printed by Perkins & Marvin, 1839.

Forrer, Leonard. *Biographical Dictionary of Medallists*. London, England: Spink & Son, Ltd., 1923.

Goldstein, Erik, and David McCarthy. "The Myth of the Continental Dollar." *The Numismatist*, January 2018.

Goldstein, Erik. "The Myth of the Continental Dollar, Part 2." *The Numismatist*, July 2018.

Gouge, William M. *A Short History of Money and Banking in the United States*. Philadelphia, PA: 1833.

Grafton, John. *The American Revolution: A Picture Sourcebook*. New York, NY: Dover Publications, 1975.

Greeley, Horace. *The American Conflict: A History of the Great Rebellion. . . .* Hartford, CT: O.D. Case & Company, 1864.

Greene, Albert G., ed. *Recollections of the Jersey Prison-Ship: Taken, and Prepared for Publications, from the Original Manuscript of the Late Captain Thomas Dring, of Providence, R.I., One of the Prisoners*. New York, NY: P.M. Davis, 1831. Revised and re-edited edition by Henry B. Dawson, Morrisania, NY, 1865.

Hardie, James, A.M. *The Description of the City of New York*. New York, NY: Samuel Marks, 1827.

Hayward, John. *A Gazetteer of the United States of America*. Philadelphia, PA: Published by the author, 1854.

Historical Magazine, The. Morrisania, NY. Issues in Series 1, 2, and 3, 1850s–1860s.

Hodder, Michael. "The Continental Currency Coinage of 1776: A Trial Die and Metallic Emission Sequence." *The American Numismatic Association Centennial Anthology.* Colorado Springs, CO: American Numismatic Association, 1991.

Jordan, Louis E. and Robert H. Gore Jr. Numismatic Endowment, University of Notre Dame, Department of Special Collections. Website compiled and maintained by Louis E. Jordan.

Journal of the Proceedings of Congress. Various issues. Washington, D.C., 1775 to date.

Kenney, Richard D. *Early American Medalists and Die-Sinkers Prior to the Civil War.* New York, NY: Wayte Raymond Publications, 1954.

Kleeberg, John M. "The Continental Dollar; British Medals or American Coins?" *Journal of Early American Numismatics,* December 2018.

Knapp, Samuel L. *Life of Lord Timothy Dexter.* Newburyport, MA: John G. Tilton; also Boston: Wm. J. Reynolds & Co., 1852.

Kouwenhoven, John A. *The Columbia Historical Portrait of the City of New York.* Garden City, NY: Doubleday & Co., Inc., 1953.

Lasser, Joseph R. "Continental Currency Signing Patterns——.Why, When, and How." *The Numismatist,* May 1975.[1]

Leonard, Robert D. "On the Origin of the Continental Dollar." *E-Sylum,* October 2012.

——. "Reader Thoughts on Continental Dollar Origins." *E-Sylum,* November 5, 2017.

Lossing, Benson John. *The Pictorial Field-Book of the American Revolution.* New York, NY: Harper & Brothers, 1855.

——. *History of New York City.* New York, NY: The Perine Engraving and Publishing Co., 1884.

——. *The Empire State: A Compendious History of the Commonwealth of New York.* New York, NY: Funk & Wagnalls, 1887.

Mason, Ebenezer, Jr. "Continental Paper Money and Its Imitations." *Mason's Coin and Stamp Collectors' Magazine,* Philadelphia, PA: 1871.

McBride, David P. "Linked Rings: Early American Unity Illustrated." *The Numismatist,* January 1979.

McCarthy, David. "More Continental Dollar Research." *E-Sylum,* July 20, 2018.

McCusker, John J. *Money and Exchange in Europe and America, 1600–1775: A Handbook.* Chapel Hill, NC: University of North Carolina Press, 1978.

McDowell, Christopher R. *Abell Buell and the History of the Connecticut and Fugio Coinages.* Colonial Coin Collectors Club, 2015.

Mossman, Philip L. *Money of the American Colonies and Confederation: A Numismatic, Economic & Historical Correlation.* New York, NY: American Numismatic Society, 1993.

——. "The American Confederation: The Times and Its Money." *Coinage of the American Confederation Period*. New York, NY: American Numismatic Society, 1996.

Newman, Eric P. "The 1776 Continental Currency Coinage." *The Coin Collector's Journal*, July–August 1952.

——. "Varieties of the Fugio Cent." *The Coin Collector's Journal*, July–August 1952.

——. "Counterfeit Continental Currency Goes To War." *The Numismatist*, January 1957.

——. "The Successful British Counterfeiting of American Paper Money During the American Revolution." *British Numismatic Journal*, 1958.

——. "The Continental Dollar of 1776 Meets Its Maker." *The Numismatist*, August 1959.

——. "Nature Printing on Colonial and Continental Currency." *The Numismatist*, February 1964, etc.

——. "Sources of Emblems and Mottoes." *The Numismatist*, December 1966.

——. "Benjamin Franklin and the Chain Design." *The Numismatist*, January 1983.

——. "Unusual Printing Features on Early American Paper Money." *Money of Pre-Federal America*. New York, NY: American Numismatic Society, 1991.

——. *The United States Fugio Copper Coinage of 1787*. Ypsilanti, MI: Jon Lusk, 2007.

——. *Early Paper Money of America*. 5th edition. Iola, WI: Krause Publications, 2008.

Newman, Eric P. and Maureen Levine. "18th Century Writings on the Continental Currency Dollar Coin." *The Numismatist*, July 2014.

Newman Numismatic Portal. Internet site with free access to many numismatic publications, an essential resource.

Nipper, Will. *In Yankee Doodle's Pocket: The Myth, Magic, and Politics of Early America*. Conway, AR: 2008.

Numismatic News. Various issues. Iola, WI, and Stevens Point, WI: 1952 to date.

Numismatist, The. Various issues. Colorado Springs, CO (and other addresses): American Numismatic Association, 1891 to date.

Orosz, Joel J. *The Eagle That Is Forgotten: Pierre Eugène Du Simitière, Founding Father of American Numismatics*. Wolfeboro, NH: Bowers and Merena Galleries, 1988.

Phelps, Richard H. *Newgate of Connecticut; Its Origin and Early History*. American Publishing Co., 1876; reprinted in 1927 by Clarence W. Seymour, Hartford, CT.

Phillips, Henry, Jr. *Historical Sketches of American Paper Currency*. Roxbury, MA: W. Elliot Woodward, 1866.

Prime, W.C. *Coins, Medals, and Seals*. New York, NY: Harper & Brothers, 1861.

Raguet. Condy. *A Treatise on Currency and Banking*. London, England: 1839.

Raymond, Wayte. *Standard Catalogue of United States Coins and Paper Money* (titles vary). New York, NY: Scott Stamp & Coin Co. (and others), 1934 to 1957 editions.

Richardson, John M. "A Numismatic Medley in Brown Paper." *The Numismatist*, January 1935.

Rodriguez, Robert. "Rob Rodriguez on the Continental Dollar." *E-Sylum*, October 29, 2017.

The Resolute Americana Continental Dollar Collection. Sarasota, FL: Numismatic Guaranty Corporation, 2017.

Schilke, Oscar G., and Raphael E. Solomon. *America's Foreign Coins: An Illustrated Standard Catalogue with Valuations of Foreign Coins with Legal Tender Status in the United States 1793–1857*. New York, NY: Coin and Currency Institute, Inc., 1964.

Scott, Kenneth. "A British Counterfeiting Press in New York Harbor, 1776." *The New-York Historical Society Quarterly*, April–July 1955.

——. *Counterfeiting in Colonial America*. New York, NY: Oxford University Press, 1957.

Sparks, Jared. *The Life of George Washington*. Boston, MA: Tappan and Dennet, 1843.

Shevlin, Jeff. "Continental Dollar Restrikes." *So-Called Dollar Collectors' Club Journal*, Volume 1, Issue 1.

Spiro, Jacob N. "Papers Relating to the Official Destruction of Continental Currency." *Numismatic Review*, Stack's, July 1946.

Stauffer, David McNeely. *American Engravers Upon Copper and Steel*. New York, NY: The Grolier Club of the City of New York, 1907.

Stokes, I.N. Phelps. *The Iconography of Manhattan Island: 1498–1909*. New York, NY: Robert H. Dodd, various dates in the 1910 and 1920s.

Sumner, William Graham. *A History of American Currency*. New York, NY: Henry Holt & Co., 1874.

——. *The Financier and the Finances of the American Revolution*. Vols. I and II. New York, NY: Dodd, Mead and Co., 1891.

Thacher, James, M.D. *Military Journal, During the American Revolutionary War, from 1775 to 1783*. Cottons & Barnard, 1823.

Describing the Events and Transactions of this Period. Hartford, CT: Silas Andrus & Son, 1854.

Vlack, Robert A. *Early American Coins*. Johnson City, NY: Windsor Research Publications, Inc., 1965.

Watson, John F. *The Annals of Philadelphia, and Pennsylvania, in the Olden Time*. Philadelphia, PA: Copyright by Elijah Thomas, 1857

Webster, Pelatiah. "An Essay on Free Trade and Finance." *Political Essays on the Nature, Money, Public Finances, and Other Subjects: Published during the American War and continued up to the present year 1791*. Philadelphia, PA: 1791.

About the Author

Q. David Bowers has been in the rare-coin business since he was a teenager in 1953, including in later times as a founder of Stack's Bowers Galleries. He has been central in showcasing at auction the greatest collections ever sold, including those of T. Harrison Garrett (for Johns Hopkins University), Ambassador and Mrs. R. Henry Norweb, Virgil M. Brand, Louis E. Eliasberg, Harry W. Bass Jr., and D. Brent Pogue—accomplishments unmatched in professional numismatics. He is a recipient of the Pennsylvania State University College of Business Administration's Alumni Achievement Award (1976); he has served as president of the American Numismatic Association (1983–1985) and president of the Professional Numismatists Guild (1977–1979); he is a recipient of the highest honor bestowed by the ANA (the Farran Zerbe Award); he was the first ANA member to be named Numismatist of the Year (1995); and one of only a few living people enshrined in the Numismatic Hall of Fame.

Bowers is a recipient of the highest honor given by the Professional Numismatists Guild and has received more Book of the Year Awards and Best Columnist honors given by the Numismatic Literary Guild than any other writer. In July 1999, in a poll published in *COINage*, "Numismatists of the Century," he was recognized as one of six living people in this list of just eighteen names. He is the author of more than 60 books, hundreds of auction and other catalogs, and several thousand articles, including columns in *Coin World* (since 1961, the longest-running column in numismatic history) and *The Numismatist*.

Bowers is a trustee emeritus of the New Hampshire Historical Society and a fellow of the American Antiquarian Society, the American Numismatic Society, and the Massachusetts Historical Society. For 18 years he was a guest lecturer at Harvard University. He has been a key consultant for the Smithsonian Institution since the 1960s, the Treasury Department, and the U.S. Mint, and he is research editor of *A Guide Book of United States Coins* and senior editor of the *Deluxe Edition* of the *Guide Book of United States Coins* ("*Mega Red*"). For Whitman Publishing, he has been the numismatic director since 2003. In Wolfeboro, New Hampshire, he is on the Board of Selectmen and is the town historian.

Credits and Acknowledgments

$\mathcal{T}$he author expresses appreciation to the following for help through personal contact and/or published research over a long period of years:

American Antiquarian Society, American Numismatic Association, American Numismatic Society, Julia H. Casey, *Coin World*, John Dannreuther, John J. Ford Jr., David Gladfelter, Thomas K. DeLorey, DM Rare Coins, HathiTrust, Heritage Auctions, Wayne Homren, William Hyder, John Kraljevich, Joseph R. Lasser, Library of Congress, Christopher R. McDowell, New-York Historical Society, Rob Rodriguez, Jeff Shevlin, Stack's Bowers Galleries, David M. Sundman, and Ray Williams.

IMAGE CREDITS

Unless otherwise noted below, images are from the personal archives of the author. Images are credited by page number. Where multiple images are depicted on a page, they are numbered left to right, top to bottom.

Chapter 1: Page xiv, Library of Congress. Page 6, Library of Congress. Page 7, Library of Congress. Page 8.2, Library of Congress. Page 9.1, Library of Congress. Page 12, Library of Congress. Page 13, Whitman archives. Page 14, New York Public Library. Page 16–17, Library of Congress. Page 18, Library of Congress. Page 22.1–22.2, Stack's Bowers Galleries. Page 23, Stack's Bowers Galleries. Page 24.1–24.6, Stack's Bowers Galleries. Page 25, New York Public Library.

Chapter 2: Page 28, Library of Congress. Page 44, Library of Congress.

Chapter 3: Page 46, Everett Collection / Shutterstock. Page 54.1–54.2, Eric P. Newman Numismatic Education Society. Page 78.1–78.2, Eric P. Newman Numismatic Education Society. Page 90.1–90.2, Eric P. Newman Numismatic Education Society. Page 93.1–93.2, Eric P. Newman Numismatic Education Society. Page 112.1–112.2, Eric P. Newman Numismatic Education Society. Page 117.1–117.2, Eric P. Newman Numismatic Education Society. Page 138.1–138.2, Eric P. Newman Numismatic Education Society. Page 161.3, Library of Congress.

Chapter 4: Page 164, Library of Congress. Page 166, Library of Congress. Page 169, New York Public Library. Page 173, New York Public Library.

Chapter 5: Page 176, New York Public Library. Page 180, Whitman archives. Page 181, New York Public Library. Page 184, Everett Historical / Shutterstock.

Chapter 6: Page 190, Library of Congress. Page 194, Eric P. Newman Numismatic Education Society.

Appendices: Page 214, Everett Historical / Shutterstock. Page 230, Whitman archives. Page 231, Whitman archives. Page 234, Whitman archives. Page 235, Whitman archives. Page 238.1–238.2, Heritage Auctions. Page 239.1–239.2, Heritage Auctions. Page 240.1–240.2, Heritage Auctions. Page 241.1–241.2, Heritage Auctions. Page 242.1–242.2, Heritage Auctions. Page 243.1–243.2, Heritage Auctions. Page 244.1–244.4, Heritage Auctions. Page 245.1–245.2, Heritage Auctions. Page 246.1–246.2, Heritage Auctions. Page 247.1–247.4, Heritage Auctions. Page 248.1–248.2, Heritage Auctions. Page 253.1–253.4, Stack's Bowers Galleries. Page 254.1–254.2, Stack's Bowers Galleries. Page 257, Library of Congress. Page 258, Stack's Bowers Galleries.

INDEX OF MOTTOES